FROM MISHNAH TO SCRIPTURE

Number 67

FROM MISHNAH TO SCRIPTURE
The Problem of the Unattributed Saying
With Special Reference to the Division of Purities

by
Jacob Neusner

FROM MISHNAH TO SCRIPTURE
The Problem of the Unattributed Saying
With Special Reference to the Division of Purities

by
Jacob Neusner

Scholars Press
Chico, California

FROM MISHNAH TO SCRIPTURE
The Problem of the Unattributed Saying
With Special Reference to the Division of Purities

by

Jacob Neusner

Library of Congress Cataloging in Publication Data

Neusner, Jacob, 1932–
From Mishnah to Scripture.

(Brown Judaic studies ; no. 67)
1. Mishnah. Tohorot (Order)—Criticism, interpretation,
etc. I. Title. II. Series
BM506.T73N477 1984 296.1'23066 84–10527
ISBN 0-89130-749-4 (pbk.)

Printed in the United States of America
on acid-free paper

For

Anthony J. Saldarini

CONTENTS

PREFACE

The history of the formation of Judaism, attested by the successive documents of the rabbinic canon from the Mishnah, ca. A.D. 200, through the Talmud of Babylonia, ca. A.D. 500-600, rests on two pillars.

First, the distinct documents themselves testify to the opinions held by the group of redactors who collected and organized those compositions. So we may confidently assign to a given place, time, and circle of rabbinical philosophers, the viewpoints paramount in the book that they wrote. That conception is the sole premise of solid work.

Second, within the diverse documents sayings are attributed to specific authorities and stories are told about them. Whether or not a report of something said and done by such an authority permits us to attribute to the place, time, and circle of that authority the opinions and actions reported in the saying or story presents a considerable problem. But the data constituted by the attribution do raise possibilities that their absence would have denied us.

The several components of the canon of Judaism contain another sort of saying, one not attributed to a named authority, and a different type of story, one not focused on a specific figure of exemplary standing. This book takes up the issue of how we are to situate unattributed sayings contained in the first document of Judaism, the Mishnah. We want to know whether and how we may determine to what place, time, or circle an unattributed saying testifies. We ask whether a saying without an attribution to a given authority differs in its fundamental character or function from one that bears an attribution. At hand, therefore, is a historical problem. The problem of situating or locating the historical provenance of sayings lacking named authorities may be framed in two distinct ways.

First of all, unattributed sayings form no distinct group, exhibiting characteristics different from attributed ones. Hence we cannot generalize at all concerning the historical or mythic traits of sayings simply because they bear no names. That, after much labor, will turn out to be the result of this inquiry into the unattributed sayings in the Mishnah.

Second, unattributed sayings do constitute a separate group, with traits of its own. These sayings belong together as a single stratum, to be situated historically at some point in the formation of the ideas and laws now written down in the Mishnah.

This second conception, treating unattributed sayings as an identifiable group and maintaining that, because a saying lacks a name, it is either very late and redactional (a position not widely held) or very early and fundamental to the ideational structure of the Mishnah, indeed a link to the "Oral Torah" of rabbinic myth, is a commonplace. Hence we had best spend some time unpacking the components of the conception to the obliteration of which this book is devoted. Let us take up, first, the historical allegation about unattributed sayings. We are faced with three choices.

1. Unattributed sayings go "way back," that is, to the pre-history of the system of rigorous thought that reaches final expression in the Mishnah.

2. Unattributed sayings come at the very end of the process and form a final layer of ordering and completion, imposed by the ultimate framers of the Mishnah itself.

3. Unattributed sayings must be located somewhere between the beginning (1) and the end (2), that is, in terms of their content and place in the unfolding logical order of the Mishnah's several discrete modules of inquiry.

I can think of no other choices. The first two possibilities do not permit detailed search for relevant data. We cannot test whether they are right or wrong. The reason is diverse. In the case of the former of the two, we have no data from the pre-history of the Mishnaic system. So we cannot test the unknown against the known. In the case of the latter, we beg the question if we suppose that the point of formulation of a saying defines also the moment of its conception. People thought things before what they thought was worded for formulation and transmission in the larger Mishnaic document now in our hands. Some of what they thought can have reached the framers of the Mishnah long afterward. So even though an unattributed saying clearly defines the logical framework within which all other sayings of a given unit of thought find their place and so appears to come at the end and climax of the labor of organization and formulation, that fact does not settle the question. And there are no other facts that permit us to determine when an unattributed saying stands at the end of the process, and where it stands at the outset. It is the third possibility that demands a detailed sifting and sorting out of the facts of the matter, and that is what I propose to provide in this book -- that and one other. We have also to ask about the extent and importance of the problem of the unattributed saying to begin with. As we shall see, in the Mishnah the problem proves paltry and trivial. The problem of unattributed sayings turns out to have been wrongly formulated and vastly overstated. I shall correctly formulate it and reduce it to its proper proportion. So, to conclude: the principal problem at hand is to discover exactly what people wish to allege about the character and antiquity of the unattributed sayings, both in general and in the Mishnah in particular. The complexity of the allegations makes it difficult to understand precisely what people propose to say.

I have tried in what follows to sort out the several major allegations and to test them against the evidence of the division at hand:

1. Do unattributed sayings form a single classification, defined by absence of attributions?

2. Do these sayings "go way back?"

3. Are they part of "The Oral Torah?"

I decided to write this book because of the insistence of two colleagues, teachers, and dear friends, Professor Anthony J. Saldarini, Boston College, and Professor Martin Hengel, University of Tuebingen. In his book reviews and other writings Saldarini has repeatedly asked for a systematic study of the matter at hand.[1] In letters to me, time and again, Hengel has pursued the same issue.

In point of fact I thought that, in my History of the Mishnaic Law of Purities (Leiden, 1974-1977) I-XXII, I had answered this question. But I realize now that while I had assembled the pertinent data, I had never explicitly and in a cogent way addressed the issue head on. And even if I had, I have to concede it is asking too much to expect people to work their way through twenty volumes of text-analysis and commentary so as to find the answers I propose, let alone to compose them into a single coherent answer. Since a decade has passed from the appearance of my earliest discussions of the matter and the question continues to flutter about, I decided to assemble what I had said into a systematic and complete account of the matter.

In fact, my original view was that I closed the question, for the Mishnah (and, by the way, the Tosefta, which is thoroughly considered in the catalogues at hand as well), in the work on Purities. That is why, in the other four parts of the history (A History of the Mishnaic Law of Holy Things [1978-1979] I-VI, A History of the Mishnaic Law of Women [1970-1980] I-V, A History of the Mishnaic Law of Appointed Times [1980-1981] I-V, and A History of the Mishnaic Law of Damages [1983-1985] I-V) I treated the question rather casually. I simply listed unattributed sayings within other rubrics entirely and subordinated the question, often dismissing it with a system of sigla -- asterisks, crosses, and the like -- which permitted me to point to what seemed to me ineffably obvious. While I cannot now restate step by step the results of the analysis of the data in those other four parts, I do wish to make explicit the conclusions spread across the twenty volumes of Purities' source analysis. In this way I can show precisely the state of the question as the facts of the Mishnah's largest division dictate the answer. People interested in pursuing the matter along these same lines will find the wherewithal for their inquiry in the appropriate places in the other four parts of the entire History.[2]

This book finds its place in a larger exercise I have undertaken. I have decided to make available to a broad new audience some small part of the results reached in works of mine now in print for from ten to twenty years and more. The other volumes in this modest project are these: The Jews in Talmudic Babylonia. A Political History (New York, 1984: Ktav), which summarizes some parts of the opening chapter of the results of my History of the Jews in Babylonia (Leiden, 1966-1970) II-V, and Judaism, Christianity, and Zoroastrianism in Talmudic Babylonia (New York, 1984: Ktav), which does the same for other components of those same chapters, and The Rabbinic Traditions about the Pharisees before 70. A Students' Edition (New York, 1984: Ktav), a simple abbreviation of the results of the original three volumes. In addition, the third printing of my History of the Jews in Babylonia. I. The Parthian Period (Chico, 1984: Scholars Press for Brown Judaic Studies) has just now appeared. In these ways bits and pieces of researches that have stood the test of time go forth to a new generation of young scholars. My hope, as always, is that others will build upon, and so make obsolete, the results I have attained.

In addition to thanks to Professors Saldarini and Hengel, I am indebted for everyday counsel on this project to Professor William Scott Green, University of Rochester, as well as to my dear colleagues, Professor Ernest S. Frerichs, Co-director of the Program in Judaic Studies at Brown University, and Professor Wendell S. Dietrich, Member of the Executive Committee of the Program.

Since Brown University has provided a generous fund to support certain aspects of my scholarly work, I thank also President Howard R. Swearer, Provost Maurice Glicksman, Associate Provost Kathryn Spoehr, Dean of the Graduate School Mark Schupack, and Dean of the College Harriet Sheridan. The renewed appreciation, within the University, for works of scholarship -- as distinct from politics and personalities (also again appreciated, by the way) -- is to be noted. In no university today can scholars take for granted respect, understanding, appreciation, and support for systematic and sustained works of learning -- research and scholarship. It is a struggle every day to insist that knowing counts and that learning matters in universities. Barbarians and know-nothings substitute feeling for thought, make things up as they go along and call their private invention knowledge. So the fight is every day. But we do not always lose, and, when we win, the world gains in reasoned illumination. In Brown University I did not always find these academic virtues, but I do now, and I am glad and take nothing for granted.

J.N.

Program in Judaic Studies
Brown University
Providence, Rhode Island, U.S.A.

April 16, 1984
14 Nisan 5744
Erev Pesah

Notes

[1]Saldarini's principal statements on the problem of the unattributed saying are as follows: "Form Criticism in Rabbinic Literature," Journal of Biblical Literature 1977, 96:257-274, esp. pp. 268-9, where he proposes the possibility that the logical order among attributed and anonymous sayings may be redactional; and cf. also JBL 1976, 95:149-151; Journal of the American Academy of Religion 1981, p. 724; and Catholic Biblical Quarterly 1973, 35:258-261, esp. p. 260. At that early point (1973), Saldarini noted -- quite fairly -- that "anonymous traditions... are probably needed to give us a full picture of pre-70 A.D. Pharisaic Judaism. In the past attempts have been made to isolate early groups of materials, by Ginzberg, Albeck, Epstein, and others, but this work must be expanded and verified by a consistent methodology."

[2]As of this writing, Professor Alan J. Avery-Peck is working on a History of the Mishnaic Law of Agriculture. Precisely how he will treat the unattributed sayings in the first division of the Mishnah and the conclusions he will reach I cannot say.

INTRODUCTION

What makes rabbinic Judaism rabbinic is the attribution of authoritative statements to named, individual rabbis. Across the far reaches of the rabbinic canon of late antiquity -- from the first century to the seventh of the Common Era -- we meet a vast population of authorities, in whose names most sayings are handed on. From the first document of the rabbinic canon, the Mishnah (ca. A.D. 200) to the last, the Talmud of Babylonia (ca. A.D. 500-600), the entire sequence of documents exhibits a single, characteristic interest in who said what.

At the same time, the literature at hand includes statements not attributed to a particular authority. These occur in one of three ways.

First, most unattributed statements stand side by side with attributed ones and take a position contrary to the one bearing a particular rabbis's name. In this case, the unattributed saying does not belong to a named rabbi, but it certainly does belong to the setting in time and circumstance of the rabbi named alongside.

Second, a fair portion of the editorial work of forming a given document will stand by itself, lacking all attribution. Extreme examples are the two Talmuds, both of which emerge out of a vast and systematic editorial project in which available materials are recast into the systematic and rigorous discussions now in our hands. But other examples of the same labor, carried on anonymously, of constructing cogent documents out of bits and pieces of assigned sayings, derive from the Mishnah, the Tosefta, and various other collections. The editorial authority of the Mishnah bears an assignment to "Our Holy Rabbi," that is, Judah the Patriarch, ca. 170-220, and of the Tosefta to Hiyya, a younger contemporary. To Ashi, a named authority of the fifth century, the work of constructing the Talmud of Babylonia is attributed.

Third, sayings and even entire pericopae (completed units of thought) may stand entirely on their own. These, strictly speaking, bear no attributions nor indications of authorship of any kind, since, by definition, they do not include reference to named rabbis, on the one side, nor belong within the editorial province of the large-scale reaction of complete documents, e.g., the Mishnah, the Tosefta, or the Talmuds, on the other. This book takes up the problem of this third sort of unattributed saying.

Let me explain the problem at hand and spell out how I propose to solve it.

First, I take up only one document of the rabbinic canon, the Mishnah. The reason is that the Mishnah stands at the head of the line of writings. If we are to begin somewhere, it might as well be at the beginning.

Second, I deal with only one division of the Mishnah, namely, the division of Purities, which forms 26% of the whole. In my judgment what we shall see in the division at hand, on which the work is already done (in my History of the Mishnaic Law of Purities [Leiden, 1974-1977] I-XXII), will suggest the state of affairs for the Mishnah as a whole.

Third, what I want to investigate is the place of the unattributed saying in the larger ideational structure of the dozen tractates of the division at hand.

Let me explain what I mean by "ideational structure," since the concept may not prove immediately familiar. In my History of the Mishnaic Law I have traced the unfolding of the legal conceptions of the tractates of five of the Mishnah's six divisions. In each case I was able to show which ideas came first and which came later on, so that, in the end, the development of a tractate's thought about its topic, the history of ideas on that topic as they unfolded from one period to the next, became clear. In most instances, specifically, I could show that the topic at hand was worked out through four successive periods of thought, one ending at 70, the next running from the destruction of the Temple in 70 to the Bar Kokhba War in 132, the third from the end of that war for roughly a generation, 135-170, and the last from that time to the closure of the Mishnah, ca. 170 to ca. 210. The dates are, of course, mere guesses, but the division by strata marked out by the names of authorities who lived in a given period stands quite firm. To be sure, some tractates got under way before others, so that we have tractates that appear to have commenced their history before 70, while the ideas in other tractates seem to have taken shape only after 135. But where we do have a clear picture of the strata marking off the development of the ideas, on a given topic, of a tractate, we may then ask the fundamental question about the place, within the strata or in relationship to the identified strata, of ideas contained within (and only within) unattributed sayings.

Now what, exactly, do we want to know about these unattributed sayings? These are the questions:

1. What proportion of the whole ideational system of a tractate, viewed in its strata is represented by the unattributed saying? Is it large or small, dominant, and generative or subordinate and a matter of detail?

2. What is the relationship between ideas framed wholly in unattributed sayings and those given in the names of particular authorities and generations?

3. Where we find ideas or facts taken for granted in unattributed sayings that stand at the logical beginning of the unfolding of principles and propositions in a given tractate, whence do those deeply imbedded and generative ideas or facts derive?

4. Specifically, do unattributed ideas or facts form a bridge from the Mishnah backward to Scripture? That is to say, is it possible to speculate that, in unattributed sayings (some if not all of them) we gain access to ideas or facts that stand even prior to the beginning of the formative history of the ideas presented in the unfolding of the tractates at hand? Can such ideas even have precipitated the reflection that led to the speculation now before us in the tractate at hand?

The reason that this fourth proposition must come under analysis derives partly from the logic of the problem at hand, for the Mishnah is a document referring back to facts of an authoritative and revealed code and is incomprehensible without those available facts. The Mishnah, specifically, relates to the Mosaic revelation. But the fourth proposition is important for an extrinsic consideration as well. It derives from the allegation that, when a saying stands above and beyond all dispute, the reason is that that saying is "very old."

The undisputed saying lacks named authority and for all parties concerned in it, and so forms part of the pre-history of the Mishnah itself. The sources of that view, extrinsic to the Mishnah but universally imputed to its unattributed sayings, prove diverse, but one important stream flows from the following passage:

B. Said R. Yose, "At first there were dissensions in Israel only in the court of seventy in the hewn-stone chamber in Jerusalem.

C. "And there were other courts of twenty-three in the various towns of the land of Israel, and there were [two] courts of three judges each in Jerusalem, one on the Temple mount, and one on the Rampart.

D. "[If] someone needed to know what is the law, he would go to the court in his town.

E. "[If] there was no court in his town, he would go to the court in the town nearest his.

F. "If they had heard the law, they told him, If not, he and the most distinguished member of that court would come up to the court which was on the Temple mount.

G. "If they had heard the law, they told them. And if not, they and the most distinguished member of that group would come to the court which was on the Rampart.

H. "If they had heard, they told them, and if not, these and those would go to the high court which was in the hewn-stone chamber.

I. "The court which was in the hewn-stone chamber, even though it consists of seventy-one members, may not fall below twenty-three.

J. "[If] one of them had to go out, he looks around to see whether there will be twenty-three left. If there will be twenty-three left, he goes out, and if not, he does not go out --

K. "unless there will be twenty-three left.

L. "And there they remained in session from the time of the daily whole-offering of the morning until the time of the daily whole-offering of the twilight.

M. "On Sabbaths and on festivals they came only to the studyhouse which was on the Temple mount.

N. "[If] a question was brought before them, if they had heard the answer, they told them.

O. "If not, they stand for a vote.

P. "[If] those who declare unclean turn out to form the majority, they declared the matter unclean. [If] those who declare the matter clean form the majority, they declared the matter clean.

Q. "From there did the law go forth and circulate in Israel.

R. "*From the time that the disciples of Shammai and Hillel who had not served their masters so much as was necessary became numerous, dissensions became many in Israel*. [Italics supplied.]

S. "And from there they send for an examine everyone who is wise and prudent, fearful of sin and of good repute, in whom people found pleasure.

T. "They make him judge in his town.

U. "Once he has been made a judge in his town, they promote him and seat him on the Rampart's court, and from there they promote him and seat him in the court of the hewn-stone chamber...."

(T. Sanhedrin 7:1)

The tale, assigned to the mid-century authority, Yose, is important to our inquiry for two reasons.

First, Yose asserts at the outset that disputes originally were limited. In earlier times the law circulated unmarred by the sort of dissension familiar in Yose's own day (and in the Mishnah itself, redacted a generation later). It was only from the time of Shammai's and Hillel's disciples that disputes became numerous.

That observation of course corresponds, second, to the simple, observable fact that nearly all disputed statements in the Mishnah occur in the names of authorities beyond the figures of Shammai and Hillel. My Rabbinic Traditions about the Pharisees before 70 (Leiden, 1971) I-III provides a complete catalogue of the relevant materials; there we see that a negligible number of disputes in the Mishnah bear the names of figures before Shammai and Hillel. A vast number appears in the names of their disciples, the two Houses (the whole of volume II, in fact!). Accordingly, Yose's observations proves congruent to the characteristics of the document at hand, the Mishnah itself.

At the same time, were we to take his statement as a matter of historical fact (which it surely is not), we should have to entertain a quite fresh proposition. It is that sayings not bearing names, hence accepted by all authorities, derive (in the main, if not in their entirety) from that golden age of authentic learning prior to, and ending with, Shammai and Hillel. Accordingly, we might be moved to postulate, what comes under dispute is late, and (more important) what does not is "early." How early, we cannot say, but surely "way back" before the first century of the common era.

That proposition need not detain us except as a reason for raising the question at hand. The question is, I repeat, exactly where in the document under study may we locate the sayings not assigned to particular authorities? And how shall we situate those sayings in the grid that begins with Scripture ("Sinai") and concludes with the publication of the Mishnah?

Admittedly, this second question is theological and not historical in character. It derives from the conviction of Judaism that the Mishnah derives from the oral Torah revealed by God to Moses "our rabbi" at Sinai and transmitted by him to the prophets and men of the great assembly, not in writing but only in processes of oral formulation and oral transmission. Hence, we see, the interest in the location of unattributed sayings in relationship to Scripture bespeaks a deeper question: shall we find in these sayings (those that go "way back") some of the marks of those memorized Torah-laws and Torah-teachings of which the myth of the dual Torah -- written and oral -- speaks?

I raise the question because it occupies people's minds, not because I find it intrinsic to the document at hand. If some people did not take the position that the unattributed sayings are "very early" (whether in formulation or in content only), and if some (fewer) did not allege that these "very early" sayings also point toward that "oral Torah" of which the rabbinic Torah-myth speaks, there would be no reason to write this book. The state of scholarly opinion and of Judaic religious conviction alike, however, not only justifies the work, but necessitates it. For theological convictions have yielded allegations as to historical facts about literary matters. Since people believe the Mishnah contains "the Oral Torah," and since they further allege that what is unattributed in the Mishnah "goes way back" "before the first century" and so may serve to transmit elements of that "oral torah," we have to frame the question of the unattributed saying in the Mishnah and answer it. Specifically, we must ask whether what people say about the unattributed saying, its importance, its fundamental character, its antiquity, is true.

We come then to the matter of how we shall investigate the issue at hand. For it surely is not enough to take up sayings one by one and speculate item by item on whether, how, and why they are either "very early" or "very late." How we shall proceed systematically and in a consistent way through the dozen tractates at hand is what now demands attention. First, let me specify the issues joined together in the question of the unattributed saying, then explain how I shall proceed. What allegations demand specification and testing against the facts of the Mishnah?

In the case of each of the tractates at hand we have to perform three specific tasks.

First, we must catalogue all of the unattributed sayings. That procedure allows us to assess the proportion of unattributed to attributed sayings in a given tractate and to characterize the corpus of the unattributed sayings, so to see whether they constitute a corpus -- a distinct category of sayings different from attributed ones. Once catalogued, the sayings must be compared in content to those that bear attributions. (This is done in a single process.) The ones that clearly express opinions on issues moot among named authorities forthwith drop from the list. Why? Because issues on which people differed in, e.g., the mid second-century are not likely to have been definitively settled two hundred years earlier. Accordingly, those unattributed sayings clearly addressed to moot questions of the last century before the closure of the Mishnah form no part in the problem of the unattributed sayings. Rather, they take their place in the stratum in which the issue or idea addressed in the unattributed sayings is indubitably situated by the evidence of the attributed ones. So as we sort out the data of the gross catalogue, we shall see precisely what proportion of the document at hand is represented by sayings lacking all clear evidence of a time, place, circumstance, or circle of authorities, of origination, and how unattributed sayings relate to attributed ones and to the tractate as a whole.

Second, we turn to the question of the possibility that important strata of some tractates go "way back," and, along with said tractates, the unattributed sayings therein. That is the important issue, and not only for theological reasons. Can we associate a significant proportion of sayings not bearing names with that stratum of a tractate that clearly derives from authorities before the destruction of the Temple. Can we show, furthermore, that taken for granted in the earliest attributed sayings are the data provided by the unattributed ones? In the case of each tractate, we describe that part of the ideational structure that is apt to emerge from the century (or more) prior to the end of the old regime in 70, and ask about the relationship of that oldest stratum to sayings not assigned to named authorities.

Third, we proceed to move backward from the Mishnah's earliest clearly identifiable stratum of ideas to Scripture. Hence, in each case we ask, can we move from Mishnah to Scripture? And, if we can, how? And, to complete the chain of questions, with the paramount one if we do move from Mishnah to Scripture, do the unattributed sayings show us the way, or do they even stand in the path we must take?

In the case of each tractate of the dozen at hand, I proceed systematically to answer the three questions before us. At the end (in Chapter Fourteen), a summary of the results of the survey will give those answers that I am able to offer on the basis of the evidence at hand.

As I review this repertoire of questions, I find myself puzzled at the complexity of the inquiry at hand. Why should it be necessary to conduct this set of inquiries into quite distinct issues, some literary, some logical and philosophical, some theological? That is to say, why do I have to see whether unattributed sayings form a distinct category, different from attributed ones? And why do I have to ask about the place of unattributed sayings in the logical, hence ideational, structure of a tractate (which involves laying out that structure)? And why, finally, do I have to take seriously as a matter of fact the (merely) theological conviction that what is lacking an attribution represents that golden age in which the disciples learned their lessons properly, that is, that age "way back" in which Scripture reached its conclusion and the formation of the "oral Torah" culminating in the Mishnah began?

The reason for undertaking this rather confused set of separate and scarcely parallel inquiries is self-evident. A complex set of allegations about the character of unattributed statements and the status (as to "Torah") of what is contained within those statements, circulates. Quite what people think is not always made explicit, because what people are thinking is confused. So I find myself contending with an established conviction, something everyone "knows," bearing literary, logical and philosophical, and theological implications. I have to deal with the principal components of that conviction. The result then is a unitary inquiry into diverse propositions which, in these remarks, I have tried to unpack and to explain, item by item, in their distinct components. In the substantive chapters (Two through Thirteen) I then proceed, item by item, to deal with each of the three components of the regnant theory of the unattributed sayings as (1) a distinct literary corpus (2) of very old teachings that (3) comprise (part of) the Oral Torah of Moses "our rabbi" (or, for modernists, at least, Ezra!). Even at the end, in Chapter Fourteen, I have to make two quite separate statements on the outcome of the work, one of a literary character about the proportion and significance of unattributed sayings in the larger structure of the Mishnah, the other about the relationship between those sayings and the problem of whether, and how, the Mishnah relates to Scripture.

It remains to define with precision exactly what I wish to know about protean relationships between the Mishnah and Scriptures. Those relationships, complex and encompassing, have been represented by a simple-minded approach to comprise mere matters of technologies of exegesis. In fact when we ask how the Mishnah relates to Scripture and whether the Mishnah derives its ideas from Scripture, we frame in narrow and literary terms the issues of the foundations of every kind of Judaism (and, in its setting, Christianity) through the whole of the history of all forms of Judaism. But in this book I want to know only one thing: Do unattributed sayings of the Mishnah form a bridge between the earliest attributed sayings and Scripture? When we consider sayings lacking an attribution, do we examine that missing link that stands for or points to the "oral Torah?"

In the analytical chapters (Two through Thirteen) these two questions are asked in the very particular contexts of very small facts. That is as it should be. We proceed on the road back from the Mishnah to Scripture by taking very small steps, one by one. Just as God lives in the details, so truth abides in them as well. My generalizations at the end of the book then simply state in answer to the questions with which we begin the results of the accumulation of the facts that fill up the middle of the work.

When, in the pages that follow, I refer to "Yavnean" and "Ushan," I mean to speak of the period in which the sages' center at Yavneh or at Usha predominated, that is, before and after the Bar Kokhba War, respectively. The four divisions then are "pre-70," "Yavneh," "Usha," and "the time of Rabbi," bearing the dates as indicated, before 70, 70-135, 135-170, 170-210. A reference to "Part" is to my History of the Mishanic Law of Purities, as follows:

A History of the Mishnaic Law of Purities. Leiden: E. J. Brill.

I. Kelim. Chapters One through Eleven (1974).
II. Kelim. Chapters Twelve through Thirty (1974).
III. Kelim. Literary and Historical Problems (1974).
IV. Ohalot. Commentary (1975).
V. Ohalot. Literary and Historical Problems (1975).
VI. Negaim. Mishnah-Tosefta (1975).
VII. Negaim. Sifra (1975).
VIII. Negaim. Literary and Historical Problems (1975).
IX. Parah. Commentary (1976).
X. Parah. Literary and Historical Problems (1976).
XI. Tohorot. Commentary (1976).
XII. Tohorot. Literary and Historical Problems (1976).
XIII. Miqvaot. Commentary (1976).
XIV. Miqvaot. Literary and Historical Problems (1976).
XV. Niddah. Commentary (1976).
XVI. Niddah. Literary and Historical Problems (1976).
XVII. Makhshirin. (1977).
XVIII. Zabim. (1977).
XIX. Tebul Yom. Yadayim. (1977).
XX. Uqsin. Cumulative Index, Parts I-XX (1977).
XXI. The Redaction and Formulation of the Order of Purities in Mishnah and Tosefta (1977).
XXII. The Mishnaic System of Uncleanness: Its Context and History (1977).

The results of the books listed above, pertinent to the issues at hand, form the shank of this book.

The remainder of my History of the Mishnaic Law, providing data on four other divisions, follows:

A History of the Mishnaic Law of Holy Things. Leiden: E. J. Brill.
- I. Zebahim. Translation and Explanation. (1979).
- II. Menahot. Translation and Explanation. (1979).
- III. Hullin, Bekhorot. Translation and Explanation. (1979).
- IV. Arakhin, Temurah. Translation and Explanation. (1979).
- V. Keritot, Meilah, Tamid, Middot, Qinnim. Translation and Explanation. (1979).
- VI. The Mishnaic System of Sacrifice and Sanctuary. (1979).

A History of the Mishnaic Law of Women. Leiden: E. J. Brill.
- I. Yebamot. Translation and Explanation. (1979).
- II. Ketubot. Translation and Explanation. (1979).
- III. Nedarim, Nazir. Translation and Explanation. (1979).
- IV. Sotah, Gittin, Qiddushin. Translation and Explanation. (1980).
- V. The Mishnaic System of Women. (1980).

A History of the Mishnaic Law of Appointed Times. Leiden: E. J. Brill.
- I. Shabbat. Translation and Explanation. (1981).
- II. Erubin, Pesahim. Translation and Explanation. (1981).
- III. Sheqalim, Yoma, Sukkah. Translation and Explanation. (1982).
- IV. Besah, Rosh Hashshanah, Taanit, Megillah, Moed Qatan, Hagigah. Translation and Explanation. (1982).
- V. The Mishnaic System of Appointed Times. (1983).

A History of the Mishnaic Law of Damages. Leiden: E. J. Brill.
- I. Baba Qamma. Translation and Explanation. (1983).
- II. Baba Mesia. Translation and Explanation. (1983).
- III. Baba Batra, Sanhedrin, Makkot. Translation and Explanation. (1984).
- IV. Shebuot, Eduyyot, Abodah Zarah, Abot, Horayot. Translation and Explanation. (1985).
- V. The Mishnaic System of Damages. (1985).

In these studies of the named divisions, I have provided the same sort of studies of unattributed sayings and of the relationship between Scripture and the fundamental and generative presuppositions of the several Mishnah-tractates that are summarized in this book on the division of Purities. But in the subsequent studies I did not spell out issues concerning unattributed sayings. All are catalogued and related to attributed ones; all are related to the larger ideational structure of the tractates in which they occur. But in no case did I find it necessary to treat matters in the explicit detail and fully articulated argumentation that characterized the work on Purities. Indeed, writing this book, reconsidering and revising the results on Purities and spelling matters out as I do, seemed necessary because, after a decade, I found people asking exactly the questions I had already settled, for the Mishnah, in excruciating detail.

Here, then, are the results spread over the twenty-two volumes of Purities, Holy Things, Women, Appointed Times, and Damages. People who wish to make allegations, as to the traits and implications of unattributed sayings, different from the allegations offered here now will have to do what I have done and demonstrate, systematically and in detail, that the facts are other than as I have laid them out. That must mean not merely repeating things as one wants to see them, or even pointing out an alleged error in one detail or another of my picture (which surely is possible, but has never made much difference for the larger thesis). It must mean showing that

1. unattributed sayings form a distinct group from attributed ones,

2. unattributed sayings bear the generative propositions that lie at the foundations of the tractate in which they occur, and so

3. unattributed sayings (may) contain that link from the Mishnah to Scripture that stands for the mythic "oral Torah of Moses our rabbi."

Without demonstrating points (1) and (2), point (3) must remain, as a matter of fact, a mere theological curiosity, along with the convictions that the world was made in seven days and that the earth is flat. So let us debate.

CHAPTER ONE
THE ATTRIBUTED SAYING

i. The Distinction between Unattributed and Attributed Sayings

Since in the pages that follow we take with utmost seriousness the fact that a saying in the Mishnah bears the name of an authority, joined to the saying with the attributive particle, "says," we first have to ask why we should do so.

That is to say, this book rests upon the supposition that a saying that bears an attribution for that very reason falls into a quite different category from one that does not. The former serves a useful purpose in investigating the formative history of the ideas of tractates of the Mishnah. The latter may or may not serve. It is our task to find out. So I clearly suppose that joining a name to an opinion matters. Before we proceed, I must explain why I think that named sayings constitute a quite distinct type of historical evidence from those that lack names. I must explain, specifically, the reasons that in many (though not all) instances we find warrant for making use of an attribution of a saying and so assigning a given opinion to a particular stratum in the unfolding of the ideas of a tractate. I have also to spell out the reasons that in some instances we have no warrant for doing so with named sayings. When I have specified the basis for verifying or falsifying the attribution of a saying to an authority who lived in a given period among the four periods among which the authorities of the Mishnah are distributed, the status of attributed sayings will be clear. Then, in the next dozen chapters, we may turn to the problem at hand.

I have devised a simple method for distinguishing between reliable and unreliable attributions of sayings to a given period at hand. This I shall now explain. But at the outset I emphasize that we have no suitable method for distinguishing reliable from unreliable attributions of sayings to a particular named authority. So, to specify the narrow boundaries of the task, when we take attributions seriously, it is to the very limited extent that we assign what is attributed to the period in which the person to whom the saying is assigned is assumed to have lived. When we turn to unattributed sayings, we have not got even that rather minimal indication about the locus of a given opinion in the history of the unfolding of ideas of a given tractate.

ii. Falsifying or Verifying Attributions

An attribution assigns a rule or principle to a specific, named authority. What was meant by those who attributed traditions to authorities cannot be stated with certainty. While attributions are generally understood to mean that the named authority at some particular moment stated said tradition, the form of attributions calls that supposition into question. For using the present tense, 'WMR, X says, hardly implies the intent to claim that on a specific occasion, in a particular historical circumstance, the named authority made such-and-such a statement. The probable meaning simply is attributive, that is, X holds such-and-such an opinion; and the still more likely meaning is, X and his circle or school adopt or affirm such-and-such a position among several available ones. What it comes down to is that in attributing a rule or principle to a specific name, the redactors thereby intended to signify that that rule is particular and distinctive to the named authority. The position of others may not be given at all, or it may be signified under "sages say," which underlines the distinctiveness of the opinion assigned to X.

The importance of attributions for any work of analysis and historical reconstruction in the Mishnah cannot be overstated. Since (as I show in Part XXI) the several forms and formulary patterns do not yield sufficient evidence decisively to permit the assignment of an opinion in a given form to a specific redactional circle or even to a general chronological period merely because of its formal or redactional traits, we are left with only two other available significations that a rule or principle is to be set within a specific group or period of time.

The first is the claim, on the part of the rule's redactors, of exactly that fact. In assigning a saying to a given authority, those who stand behind the assignment allege that that authority holds said opinion, whether or not the opinion is also supposed to originate with, or to have been formulated by, that authority or in words approved by him. Of that matter we can never be certain.

The second, and still more important, evidence that an opinion is to be shown prior or posterior to some other is not formal (attaching a name) but substantive, specifically, if a given law takes for granted, but clearly has not been generated by, another rule or principle, then in strict logic the law comes <u>after</u> the rule or principle upon which it depends. The dependence may be of three sorts.

First, a law may take for granted an earlier and independent rule and spell out how it is to be done.

Second, the law may introduce conceptual refinements into the earlier rule, taking for granted the validity of the former and adding complexity to its gross and unrefined legal theory.

Third, the law may spell out the implications of an earlier rule, but the spelling out may exhibit clear evidence that the rule whose implications are worked out in fact is prior to the later elaboration or articulation.

All three sorts of evidence may be relied upon, through examination of the theme and substance of a rule, to indicate whether in logic it is prior or posterior to the theme or substance of some other, autonomous rule.

So the first signification is formal and chronological, in that it indicates someone thinks saying X was stated by authority A, who lived before authority B, to whom saying Y is assigned. The second signification is substantive and logical. Saying Y depends upon the facts and principle of saying X and, in its contingency, testifies to the (logical) availability of saying X. <u>Where, as I shall now explain, X/Y = A/B, that is, the sequence of logical steps by which sayings are arranged corresponds to the sequence of chronological order in which authorities to which the aforementioned sayings are attributed, there we</u>

have a basis for verifying or falsifying the relative order, in chronology and not only in logic, claimed by attributions of sayings to named authorities. Let me spell this out, with a number of concrete examples, since it is somewhat abstract as I have just now expressed it. The basic idea is simple and the logic behind it not at all complicated.

We ask, to what degree may we rely upon attributions of opinions to specific authorities in working out the main chronological periods into which the law may be divided, therefore in reconstructing the history of the law as a whole? The sole decisive answer will have to derive from the substance of the law.

iii. The Case of Mishnah Tractate Kelim

We begin with a negative instance, a test of falsification, the sole such item in our tractate. In M. Kel. 17:5, Meir and Yohanan b. Nuri supply explanations about the reference to pomegranates of Bad'an. Aqiba then explicity cites the language used by each and holds that both are right. Since Aqiba is presumed to have flourished in 100-130, that is, middle and later Yavnean times, as a contemporary and then successor of Eliezer and Joshua, on the one side, and teacher of the latest Yavneans and early Ushans (ca. 135-160), on the other, he should not be cited as coming after and referring to the language of Meir, surely an Ushan, and Yohanan b. Nuri, a figure whose traditions seem to belong to both the late Yavnean and the early Ushan periods. The first assignment of Meir to Usha is based upon the fact that all his traditions for our tractate, except this one, are cited along with those of other Ushans, never with Yavneans. The materials of Aqiba, with the present exception, in our tractate are cited solely with Yavneans, never with Ushans; Yohanan b. Nuri, as just said, is in between. It therefore is difficult to explain why Aqiba should be represented as coming after and commenting on opinions of authorities surely later and probably younger than he. To be sure, it is possible to explain the phenomenon away.

But that is not the point. It is scarcely persuasive evidence that materials which may be shown by logical analysis of theme and substance to come early have been accurately attributed to authorities who may be shown through the associations of their respective sets of traditions also to come early in the history of the law. In the present instance the substance of what is assigned to Meir, Yohanan b. Nuri, and Aqiba is of little consequence. They gloss an established rule, and their opinions do not exhibit a relationship of posteriority or priority to one another. But, as I said, this case hardly confirms the supposition that the materials are attributed according to a disciplined chronological scheme. We cannot rely on the present example to demonstrate that opinions which come earlier are normally assigned to equivalently early authorities and proceed to reconstruct the chronological periods according to which the law unfolded. That is why the example is so precious. It shows the possibility of falsification.

Let us now speak of logical and chronological tests of verification. What is probative that the temporal order of attributions is generally sound is this: in every instance in Kelim, except that just cited, in which we are able to establish the expectation that the substance of a given law is prior to that of another, closely related rule, the earlier rule also will be assigned to an earlier authority, the later rule to a later authority. Every attestation, for example, in which a later authority claims to have knowledge of what is said in the name of an earlier authority, produces a single progression: the opinion attributed to the later authority also depends upon and refines the substance of the opinion attributed to the earlier authority. Consequently, in the attestations we have many dozens of evidences that the relative division of the law, in accord with the historical sequence of the circles to whom it is attributed, is reliable. In less closely related rules we do not have a single example of a law attributed to an early authority which depends upon the prior availability of a law attributed to a later authority.

iv. Examples of Thematic Attestations in Kelim

Several sorts of specific examples of thematic attestations will spell out the prima facie reliability of the attributions.

First, and least significant, let us consider a single pericope, the least likely place for glaring errors of attribution to be found (despite M. 17:5). In M. 25:7-8 we have an ideal example of how the substance of the law unfolds in accord with the sequence of the generations to which it is attributed. First we are told a general rule: all utensils are divided into an outer part, an inner part, and a holding place. (It is taken for granted that the division is consequential in terms of purity and impurity.) The contrasting rule, 25:9, is that utensils belonging to the Temple are not regarded as divided. These two rules should be regarded as paired opposites. Then we have an effort greatly to limit the applicability of the generalization. Tarfon, of Yavnean times, holds that that rule, which provides for considerable leniency in the determination of the impurity of a utensil, applies only to a large trough, which will require a holding place to be serviceable. Forthwith the applicability of the rule to all other objects has been excluded. Obviously Tarfon's opinion cannot come before the rule which he so drastically revises. Aqiba, of Yavnean times, then differs, holding that the rule applies solely to cups. The meaning is that cups are regarded as divided into three distinct units, so far as contamination is concerned. But other objects are not. Clearly, Tarfon and Aqiba may be said to differ from one another, the former saying even large, the other only small, objects enjoy the lenient ruling. Then Yose and Meir, of Ushan times, dispute one matter only, and that is, the sort of situation in which cups are regarded as composed of distinct parts. Their dispute depends wholly on Aqiba's opinion. Since, as I said, they generally are regarded as Ushans, and Tarfon and Aqiba as Yavneans, it goes without saying that the clear logical order of the substance of the sayings accords with the established chronological order of authorities to whom the rules are attributed. It would be difficult to provide more decisive evidence that the historical stratification of the law in accord with the chronological order of the names of the authorities to whom it is attributed is reliable.

Let us now turn to a problem involving both primary documents, Mishnah and Tosefta. In M. 28:2, we have a dispute between Eliezer and Joshua, with Aqiba's compromise appended, about a piece of cloth less than three-by-three handbreadths in size. Eliezer holds that, whether or not that cloth is set aside for its particular purpose, it is clean. Aqiba takes the position that what is set aside is susceptible, what is not, but merely tossed away, is insusceptible. Now in T.B.B. 6:6D we have the saying of Simeon, in a separate context and in no way corresponding to the present dispute, but pertinent to the problem of M. 27:11. He says that if a cloth is set aside for a purpose susceptible to uncleanness, it is itself susceptible; if it is set aside for a purpose which is not susceptible to uncleanness, it is unsusceptible. This opinion T.B.B. 6:6D explains the position taken by Simeon in M. 27:11. What is important is that it depends, to begin with, upon making a distinction, in reference to setting a rag aside, between doing so for a particular purpose and doing so for no purpose at all. If the primary important issue concerns whether or not a rag has been set aside, and if one holds that whatever is the case, the cloth is clean or unclean, then Simeon's opinion is meaningless. His opinion is possible only within the supposition that setting a cloth aside yields effects different from simply tossing it away. That is to say, his opinion develops the viewpoint assigned in M. to Aqiba. Keeping the cloth in readiness is important only to Aqiba; to him it indicates that the owner has some distinctive purpose in mind. Aqiba's point then is refined by Simeon, who asks about the status, as to purity, of the function or purpose for which the rag has been set aside. What is important in the present instance is this: Simeon's saying is not brought into relationship to Aqiba's. M. knows nothing about it. T. correctly assigns it with reference to M. 27:11. Accordingly, the correct order of authorities -- Yavneans, then Ushans -- is not the work of a careful redactor of a single pericope, as may be claimed of M. 27:5-8 (+9). The authorities are not placed in order at all. Only the substance of what Simeon says relates to the opinions assigned to Eliezer, Joshua, and Aqiba. And, as we see, what Simeon says follows in sequence, and entirely depends upon, the substance of the saying assigned to Aqiba.

This example, however, requires that we now introduce an important qualification. M.'s Aqiba is alleged in T. to have been Eliezer. To put it differently, the distinction introduced by Aqiba in M. is claimed in T. to be Eliezer's. T.B.B. 6:8 shows that our version of M. is the work of Judah; Meir assigns the opinions solely to Eliezer and Joshua, leaving no room for a saying for Aqiba at all. Were our task a biography of Aqiba, Joshua, or Eliezer, we should know only that the Ushans had in hand a dispute on this matter. But we should not know precisely the position taken by Eliezer, Joshua, or Aqiba, except as Meir or Judah have told us. Since they had contradictory information, the probability is that a firm tradition was unavailable. But the divisions of the laws -- first Yavneh, then Usha -- are made clear by the attributions of their substance in conformity to the order of authorities first to Yavneans, then to an Ushan (Simeon). In our consideration of the conceptual schemes of the several authorities, we have to pay close attention to the greater degree of reliability there claimed for specific attributions of traditions to specific authorities. But for the primary effort at distinguishing the legal strata, therefore the sequential development of the law, a case such as this poses no problem whatsoever. Its evidence is probative.

Our third and best example involves the relationships between opinions in documents less closely tied to one another than are Mishnah and Tosefta. Sifra, often citing Mishnah and Tosefta verbatim, is posterior to both and exhibits a somewhat more complex set of relationships to each than does Mishnah to Tosefta and vice versa. It therefore provides a still better test of the reliability of the relative order of attributions than do M. and T. In Sifra Shemini Pereq 10:5-6 we have a debate between Eliezer and Aqiba on what marks the point in the process of manufacture at which an oven becomes susceptible to uncleanness. Eliezer says the oven is susceptible even though it has not been heated. That is the primary issue. He does not explain how he will determine the susceptibility of the oven. Aqiba maintains the oven is susceptible only after it has been heated. What should follow? To an Ushan should be attributed an opinion which tells us what constitutes the completion of the manufacture of an oven, in the supposition that heating is not required. To another Ushan should be attributed an explanation of just how much heating is required for finishing an oven.

In point of fact, M. 4:4E-5:1 has Judah explain the degree of heating required for marking the susceptibility of an oven. He opposes an anonymous opinion, which also is to be assigned to the period after, and depends upon the view of, Aqiba, Further, T. B.Q. 4:2 contains opinions assigned to Simeon b. Gamaliel and Yohanan HaSandlar which take for granted that heating is what marks the susceptibility of an oven. Judah's reading of the story of Gamaliel, M. 5:6, also assumes that Gamaliel agrees the act of heating is decisive, but the interpretation of the story about Gamaliel is clearly Judah's. Others take the story to be important for another issue entirely, so we cannot know Gamaliel's position on the subject.

Meir, by contrast, ignores the issue of heating. His view is that when the oven has reached a height at which it is useful to someone -- a little girl -- it is susceptible to uncleanness. The primary tradition to be assigned to Meir probably is that height, not heating, is decisive. This fact emerges from the several later discussions of the heights of various ovens, none of which makes reference to toy ovens.

What is important here is that the substance of the opinions attributed by Sifra to Eliezer and Aqiba certainly is prior to that of the opinions attributed by M. and T. to the Ushans, Judah, Simeon, Yohanan HaSandlar, and Meir. To be sure, it might be argued that Sifra uses the names of Eliezer and Aqiba for opinions which, in fact, were primary to the names of Meir and Judah, respectively. But that will not affect the main point, which is that the relationship of opinions, earlier, then later, corresponds to the relationship of named authorities, Yavnean, then Ushan. And as I said, the contrary phenomenon is very uncommon.

Finally, we may observe that preoccupation with a single problem, expressed in varying ways, will time and again be shown to characterize a given stratum. For example, the single most interesting problem -- the degrees by which a utensil loses its original character, as marked by the decline in the virulence of uncleanness attaching to said utensil -- is shown by quite unrelated and separate attributions and attestations to constitute a problem distinctive to Usha. M. 18:5-9, 19:5, 26:6, 27:7-8, and other versions of that same sequence contain various attributions or attestations -- every one of them to or by an Ushan.

A further argument in favor of the presumptive reliability of attributions derives from the evidence that specific individual authorities tend to give internally consistent opinions. We rarely observe the attribution of contradictory rules or principles to, e.g., Aqiba. (The Talmuds take as a principal task showing how a given authority's principles are uniformly applied to diverse cases.) While not a decisive argument, that fact suggests once again that the attribution of an opinion to an authority was not random or undisciplined, but, in the main, was guided by considerations of accuracy. To be sure, we have already noticed that what is given to Yose in M. may appear in Judah's name in T. That problem is directed toward the course of transmission, not redaction. Even more strikingly, T. frequently contains revisions of the opinions given in M. to specific, early authorities. In these instances, as already observed, the theme of the ruling is firm, but the details are not.

Finally, the attribution of disputes to the Houses is a separate issue. The names of the Houses serve as a literary convention, in a measure to be determined in its own terms and not in this book, for opinions actually generated in Usha. Where we find the Houses' debating principles well-attested for the first time in the names of Ushan authorities, we have to take account of the possibility that the attribution of the matter to the Houses is pseudepigraphic. In this regard the named masters' traditions will provide the determinative criterion.

v. Conclusion

So much for sayings bearing attributions. In all instances, these sayings provide the possibility of falsification and verification. That same possibility never occurs in unattributed sayings -- by definition. Then what are we to make of them? And specifically, can we affirm that what bears no attribution is apt to "go back" or to "come earlier" than what is attributed? Can we show, to the contrary, that disputed materials derive from a later stratum in the unfolding of the history of the ideas of the tractates of the Mishnah than the undisputed ones? Can we find grounds to allege that we may relate the undisputed materials to that fundament of materials formulated and transmitted not in writing but orally, that is, "the Oral Torah?" To the data pertinent to these questions we now turn.

CHAPTER TWO
KELIM

i. Unattributed Sayings

Nearly all laws in this tractate either are attributed to a named authority, or in principle and in detailed articulation are closely tied to an attributed law, or are diametrically opposed to a tradition assigned to a specific person and so may with confidence be located in the same division as the contrary law. The list, which follows, of unattested and unassigned pericopae contains 49 items. But of these, as many as 26 may be located in a given division, Yavnean or Ushan, if not within a single circle of masters within a given division, e.g., Aqiba's or Meir's. The exegetical studies in Parts I and II thus solve the problem of the unassigned sayings by uncovering the principles exhibited by assigned ones and common to a great many of the anonymous ones.

The use of square brackets indicates an item which, while superficially without attribution to a specific authority, in fact belongs to an identifiable circle or division. We include Tosefta's as well as Mishnah's pericopes.

1. T. B.B. 1:13: Relevant to M. 1:5L-M, but no evidence of attestation or attribution.
2. T. B.Q. 2:3A-B.
3. T. B.Q. 2:5E: Whatever serves as a cover for a clay utensil is clean. + M. 3:6B, same principle.

[4. M. 2:6: A spoiled jar is clean before finished, unclean afterward. + T. B.Q. 2:6: How do we know when it split? + M. 4:3: What is a spoiled jar? But M. 4:3 surely accords with Judah + Meir, M. 4:1-2, 6.]

5. M. 2:3A-C/M. 2:7A-C: These are the clean/unclean objects among clay utensils + tray, firepan. Perhaps also M. 8:9A-C?

[6. M. 2:7D-G: A tray full of dishes -- made unclean by a creeping thing. + Overhanging rim. But perhaps Yohanan b. Nuri's opinion attests this prior rule.]

[7. M. 3:2L: A lamp whose nozzle is taken is clean, and one made of unbaked clay whose nozzle is burned by the wick is clean. The heating must be intentional -- in accord with Gamaliel + Judah, M. 5:4.]

[8. T. B.Q. 2:9D: Spoiled jar: Measure is liquid. Fits in with Ushan opinions, probably contrary to Simeon.]

9. T. B.Q. 2:9E: Cruses of Galilee, etc., are clean before firing, unclean afterward.

[10. M. 3:3-4: Breaking a clay utensil purifies it, without regard to the capacity of the sherds. We have no attributions of this important opinion, which contradicts the views of major Ushans (3:2), such as Meir, Simeon, Judah; and Yavneans, such as Aqiba and Yohanan b. Zakkai (= Eliezer b. Jacob, Nehemiah), probably also Ishmael. -- T B.Q. 2:10C. On the other hand, Simeon b. Gamaliel in T. B.Q. 4:15-16 will agree with M. 3:3-4.]

11. T. B.Q. 3:8 The presumption concerning sherds found anywhere except at the pottery-works is that they are clean.

12. M. 5:3A: The crown of a double-stove is clean.

[13. M. 5:7E-F: If one divided an oven two unequal parts, the large is unclean, the small clean. This accords with M. 5:7A-B -- vs. Meir, T. B.Q. 4:8 says if one can do the division exactly, both parts are clean. This consideration refines the earlier view.]

14. T. B.Q. 5:8B: A domestic metal hive used as a basket is clean, so too a box of bath-house attendants.

15. M. 8:9A-C: Earth-oven, etc. No clear attribution; no principles clearly seem to pertain. Gamaliel's item does not contain a principle common to these ovens. = T. B.Q.6:16, 17A.

16. M. 9:6D-M: The spindle-hook swallowed up in a spindle, etc., are not afforded protection in the tent of a corpse and can render unclean in airspace.

[17. M. 10:7-8: The legal conundrums exhibit no relationship to a named master. But the principles they illustrate all are attributed to Yavneans or Ushans. The problems certainly do not stand outside of, and before, the attributed materials.]

[18. M. 11:8A-B: All weapons of war are unclean, all ornaments of women are unclean. + T. B.M. 1:10. But Yose's gloss of M. 13:1A-B carries in its wake T. B.M. 3:1, the same problem, purifying unclean weapons of war.]

[19. T. B.M. 1:11-14: Seals are clean, metal amulets are unclean, magical bowls are clean, ornaments of a beast are clean, except the clapper which serves man. Bells found anywhere are presumed unclean, etc. But the operative principle is, What serves man? This is to be assigned to the Ushan stratum.]

20. T. B.M. 2:4: A balance of retailers with weights but not hooks or vice versa is unclean. In both cases it is useful -- a clear principle, but not necessarily sufficient evidence to assign the rule to a specific division.

[21. M. 12:2E-H: A hook of a bed-frame is unclean and of bedpoles is clean + other hooks + general rule. + T. B.M. 2:5-7: Metal objects with receptacles are unclean. These rules accord with M. 11:1, metal receptacles are unclean, so cannot be later than Usha.]

[22. M. 15:5 The shovel of grist-dealers is unclean, of storerooms is clean. But the principle is whether or not there is a receptacle, and that cannot come later than early Yavnean times.]

[23. T. B.M. 6:3: When do utensils of bone receive uncleanness? T. B.M. 7:12 assigns the issue to Simeon b. Gamaliel.]

[24. M. 16:8A-E + L: I do not see how the items + general rule, sheaths are unclean, covers are clean, can be assigned to any particular authority. The rule corresponds to, and conflicts with, M. 16:7, Yose = Judah-Aqiba, and probably belongs to at the latest to the Ushan stratum. But this cannot be demonstrated with certainty. Judah's interpolation is merely suggestive, not probative.]

[25. M. 17:8/T. B.M. 6:12, surely are Ushan, along with the attributed or attested rules.]

26. M. 17:17A-C: A receptacle of any sort is unclean. T. B.M. 7:8A: Only a normal receptacle is unclean. + T. B.M. 7:10: Unclean is only the part of a utensil which serves as a receptacle. These rulings are part of the larger set of M. 17:15-17, probably belong with the Yohanan b. Zakkai-group.]

[27. T. B.M. 8:3: Boards of a couch are clean. Frames are unclean, etc. -- various parts of a bed. T. 8:3C repeats M. 18:3F2, which certainly belongs to the time of Yose, as shown in M. 18:4.]

28. T. B.M. 9:1: A storage-bench for tailors is not used for sitting + other items. The issue of whether or not a utensil is used for sitting faces the Houses, M. 20:2. But that does not decisively place the particular rule in or before the Yavnean stratum.

29. T. B.M. 10:5: A board of tables which has sides is unclean.

30. T. B.M. 10:6: Tables used for sitting are unclean, etc.

[31. M. 20:3: A chair attached to a post is unclean and not connected to the post. One made in the post itself is unclean. + Other examples. But the Houses dispute precisely the same point. And M. 22:4 shows 20:3 to be Hillelite. + T. B.M. 11:4-5.]

[32. M. 20:5: A block fixed to the course of a wall is unclean so long as it may be removed. Once it is permanently in place, it is clean. + Other examples. But the Houses dispute the same point. + T. B.M. 11:6-7.]

[33. T. B.B. 1:1: We do not know to what M. this T. refers. If it is to M. 21:1, then it is Ushan (Yose); if to 21:3, it also is Ushan (Judah).]

34. T. B.B. 1:11-1:12:D Benches in inns are clean, benches of school-teachers are clean. If the legs are affixed, they are unclean. Bench which is separated into its components is clean, etc. These are redacted with the Houses' dispute of M. 22:E-H, but are independent of it in principle. No. 28 is relevant.

35. M. 22:8E: The seat of the stone-cutter is unclean (midras). + T. B.B. 1:13.

36. M. 22:10A-D/T. B.B. 1:14: Toilets' components -- iron frame and leather seat -- when separated still are unclean, etc.

37. M. 23:5: The fishnet is unclean because of its network bag and other nets. The reason is that they form receptacles.

38. T. B.B. 4:13: A band for an ass -- for ornament is clean, for the belly is unclean. Remnants, lengths, etc. + 4:14A: All cords of a beast are clean, for a man are clean.

[39. M. 27:1-2: The ladders of cloth, sacking, leather, wood, and clay have no attributions or attestations, other than the gloss of 27:1G (= Hezekiah/Gamaliel I) and I-K.]

[40. M. 27:3: Anything to which is attached a fabric from a category less stringent than itself is unclean, etc. But M. 27:4, Simeon's pericope, refers to M. 27:1-2, so too M. 28:7A-C refers to 27:2.]

41. T. B.B. 5:1, 2, 3, 4: Various kinds of shirts.

[42-3. M. 27:7-8: Two cases + 3 X 3 fingerbreadths which are diminished are clean, but 3 X 3 handbreadths diminished are still susceptible to corpse-uncleanness. The problem is the same as 18:5-6, 19:5, 18:8, 26:4, therefore certainly Ushan.]

44. M. 28:8B, C: An unclean cloak is not connected once most of it is torn. The thick or thin clothes are not subject to the 3 X 3 rules. + T. B.B. 5:20, 5:11. I do not see how the assignment of M. 28:8A to Simeon b. Gamaliel affects 28:8B + C, which stand apart from A.

45. M. 28:10/T. B.B. 5:15-16: Rules on the hair net.

[46. M. 29:1F/T. B.B. 5:17, T. B.B. 7:1F: Fringes and remnant lengths, Simeon b. Gamaliel's intrusion in T. B.B. 7:1 tends to set M. 28:10 and 29:1 into Ushan times, but the link is redactional, not substantive, and does not pertain to the issue of remnants, as stated here, or to the damaged net of M. 28:10. But in T. B.B. 7:5, Yose attests 29:1]

47. M. 29:6 Connected handles of cord of balances shaft of millstone, etc.

[48. T. B.B. 7:10J-L: The glass cup etc. which were perforated, above or below, are clean. Tray or bowl -- above, unclean, below, clean. If cracked + can hold hot + cold liquids, are unclean, if not, clean. M. 3:7 assigns the principle of hot/cold to Yose.]

[49. M. 30:4A-B + D-E: A small flask without the neck is unclean, the large is clean. Large flagons which have lost their necks are unclean. The mill-funnel is clean. + T. B.B. 7:11-2. M. 12:8A = T. B.B. 7:12 are not clearly assigned to a specific stratum. The principle of 30:4C, re scratching the hand, is consistent with Eleazar b. R. Sadoq in T. B.B. 7:10M-N. Yose glosses 30:4E. So assigning the set to Usha is not farfetched.]

As observed at the outset, of the 49 items in the present list, at least 26 may with some certainty be assigned to one or another of the two principal strata, Yavneh and Usha. To be sure, linking anonymous rulings to the materials belonging to specific authorities in some measure represents a subjective judgment, and still other pericopae may more properly be assigned to the unattributed corpus. Yet even making allowances for error or differences of opinion on the matter, we cannot regard the lack of attribution for a handful of items as a significant problem. For in all, our present, severely limited system of enumerating for Kelim, encompasses 272 individual items. While a great many entries include two or three or even more individual pericopae, the unattested list tends to number each unassigned pericope by itself. Even within the present rough system of enumeration, for every tradition without an attribution we have nine with names. That means our statements on the history of the law in this tractate are based on a very large sample of the whole, approximately 90%, indeed probably closer to 98%. It is for that reason that I claim the problem of the unattributed sayings to be of negligible importance. This result will recur in the following chapters. Once we have established, through the careful study of attributed materials, definitively and distinctively characteristic of a given division, generation, or authority, we find it reasonably certain to assign to that same group many more unattributed sayings. In describing the history of the Mishnaic law of purities, it follows we do not have to take account of the possibility that a vast corpus of law, deriving from endless generations before 70, now appears, still in its original formulation, in Mishnah-Tosefta and is signified by the absence of attributions to named authorities.

We do not have to take seriously the possibility that an unattributed saying may derive from the period before 70. Why not? Because the unattributed sayings in not a single instance give evidence of originating before the attributed ones. That is, in substance they in no way suggest that, as a group or individually, they are based upon principles prior to those operative at Yavneh or Usha. Their literary forms, moreover, are the same as those characteristic of the named sayings of Yavneans and Ushans. Obviously, the corpus of legal theory may go back "long before 70" and before the Houses. But the form and substance of the materials in Mishnah and Tosefta in particular certainly do not. It therefore cannot be claimed that Mishnah and Tosefta contain laws formulated long before 70 or before the time of the Houses, and that unattributed sayings preserve those early laws.

ii. Kelim Before 70

What was the state of the law about Kelim before 70? What we want to know is not whether there were laws or exegeses of pertinent Scriptures. We take for granted there were. Our problem is, to what degree are the earliest Mishnaic laws before us in Kelim founded on an antecedent heritage? and to what degree do they appear to have begun their development primarily after the destruction in A.D. 70? and are these earliest and generative facts or principles expressed in particular in unattributed sayings, as against attributed ones.

The answer to the question, Were there laws about utensils before 70? is obvious. The Temple cult was based upon Leviticus and priestly interpretations thereof. So we can hardly doubt the availability of a substantial corpus of rules on the cleanness of utensils.

On the other hand, no evidence known to me describes the shape and detailed substance of those Temple laws. The question is, to what degree do the rules of Kelim seem to be based upon the work of Yavneans, and to what degree do they seem to continue principles, if not exact formulations, laid down at some point, discernible or otherwise, before 70?

We shall first consider those principles which clearly lie at the foundations of the Yavnean rulings and disputes and which also do not seem to have been at issue among Yavneans. These, we may postulate, come at the very beginning and may go back to pre-Yavnean times.

Second, we shall ask about the laws attributed to the Houses. We cannot take for granted that attribution to the Houses means a law goes back before 70, or even before 140. Ushans quite systematically made use of the names of the Houses for mnemonic and pedagogical purposes (they are the same). It will therefore be important to examine the disputes between the Houses one by one and to ask, Are issues at hand primarily characteristic of Ushans, in which case pseudepigraphic use of the Houses' names cannot be ruled out? Or are the issues fundamentally in accord with the Yavnean or even earlier principles, demonstrably so on the basis of other evidence?

Once we have a clear picture of the principles which lie at the very foundations of our Mishnah-Tractate, we shall ask, To what degree do these principles depend upon Scripture's plain meaning or obvious exegetical requirements, and to what degree do they rest upon a substantial antecedent tradition both of Scriptural exegesis and of legal thinking? If we see evidence of a substantial development from the legal principles and ideas revealed in Scriptures to the legal principles and ideas taken for granted at Yavneh, then that period of development may be assumed, at least hypothetically, to have taken a considerable number of years. On the other hand, if we do not locate evidences of substantial change and, particularly, development from the rules of Leviticus and Numbers to the fundamental conceptions of Yavneh, we shall be unable to show a long period of legal change to have taken place from Scripture to Mishnah (Yavneh). Claims to the contrary will have to be accompanied by evidence and arguments to account for the evident absence of indications of a long period of gestation and growth, parallel to what took place in the century before us. For at any point it was possible to turn to Scripture and apply its laws to the table-fellowship, including the utensils, of a current sect. But once those laws were applied, much new legal theory and many new rulings would be generated even in the very process of their application, let alone in study and reflection.

Let us now catalogue presuppositions of rulings assigned to the Yavneh-period, hence views held before 70.

The earliest attributed law, coming before 70, concerns the division of clay utensils into an outside and inner part. Hezekiah testifies before Gamaliel the Elder that any clay utensil which has no inner part has no outer parts. Underlying that statement -- or equivalent to it -- is the conception that whatever has a receptacle is susceptible, and whatever does not is insusceptible. A third, closely-related conception is that the contained airspace of a clay utensil is contaminable as part of the inner space. The pertinent pericopae are as follows:

A. Inside-outside

1. Attributed to Hezekiah before Gamaliel the Elder (Sifra Shemini Parashah 7:5: Whatever has no inside has no outer parts among clay utensils = M. 27:1G).

2. M. 25:7-8: Utensils have an outer part, an inner part, and a holding place, which are regarded as separate from one another.

[3. M. 2:1E-F: Clay utensils are made unclean from the contact of uncleanness with their inner space but not with their outer sides. This rule is not attested at Yavneh. It is, however, the opposite of the implication of M. 25:1A/25:7-8, that utensils are divided and their parts do not affect one another. M. 2:1E-F cannot come before Hezekiah's saying, No. 1, because it spells out the implications of that saying -- but so does No. 2.]

[4. M. 10:1-3: The finger-hole is part of the utensil. This is the Temple rule of M. 25:9. + Houses, M. 9:1 vs. M. 10:1.]

B. Receptacles

1. Any sort of receptacle is susceptible (M. 17:16). The nature of receptacles and the uncleanness of utensils which have them is a given for Yavneans.

2. M. 30:2 All parties agree a receptacle is susceptible. The issue is whether it is a normal one.

3. M. 8:9D-H, M. 12:3.

4. The further implication of M. 17:16 is that flat (wooden) utensils are insusceptible.

5. M. 12:3: Gamaliel says a domestic metal basket cover is susceptible, because it forms a receptacle.

6. M. 26:2E-F: That receptacles are susceptible is taken for granted.

C. Clay Utensils are susceptible through the contamination of airspace:

1. M. 2:8C-E: Comb of water-cooler (Eliezer).

A second group of Yavnean presuppositions concerns the susceptibility of any sort of utensil. The stress is on the traits of utensils in general, not on characteristics of specific substances, which, overall, is not a predominant concern among Yavnean rulings. The principle may be stated as follows: A susceptible utensil is one which is useful and which has a distinctive trait or quality or character of its own. An insusceptible utensil is one which is useless, that is, broken. What therefore is taken for granted is that a utensil is susceptible, a non-utensil is not. Yavneans furthermore take for granted a development of this last point, a perforated utensil is regarded as broken and insusceptible.

A. What is permanently used or kept is susceptible. What is discarded is not.

1. M. 17:2.

B. <u>An autonomous, useful object is susceptible, one which has no distinctive chararacter is not susceptible</u>.

1. M. 11:8H-I; M. 11:4F-K; M. 11:7C-E.
2. M. 12:5A-E: What makes a nail a distinctive utensil? Takes for granted the fundamental principle.
3. M. 20:4: Same issue for a trough, this time turning a trough into a bench.
4. M. 22:9A-C: A wooden block, same issue. + T. B.B. 2:4.
5. M. 22:10: Occasional use <u>vs</u>. distinctive function.
6. M. 27:5: Same issue for sifter.
7. M. 12:3: Autonomous utensils are suceptible.
8. M. 12:4-5.
9. M. 5:10D-F: The oven of Ben Dina'i has to stand by itself.
10. T. B.B. 4:5: Aqiba and the sages take for granted a normal utensil is susceptible.

C. <u>A perforated or broken utensil is insusceptible</u>

1. M. 7:1: The principle is taken for granted. The issue is solely, how large a perforation?
2. M. 2:2: A sherd which serves in the way it did before breaking is susceptible. This seems a qualification of the fundamental principle that breaking is purifying.
3. M. 2:4C-E: All parties agree receptacles are susceptible.

The third important presupposition of Yavnean rulings concerns the relationship of metal to wood. If wood is subsidiary to metal, it is susceptible as metal, and even the presence of a single part made of metal, which carries out a significant function, renders the entire utensil susceptible. The presupposition is that a flat wooden object normally is insusceptible, while a flat metal object is susceptible. The evidence is as follows:

A. <u>Wood subsidiary to metal is susceptible as metal</u>

1. M. 13:7C: Joshua says he cannot explain the inherited ruling that single metal tooth makes a wooden comb susceptible. Accordingly, a flat wooden object is normally insusceptible.
2. M. 11:4: Wood plated with metal is clean.
3. T. B.M. 1:5: Halafta, Aqiba. + M. 11:6.

We have two further principles taken for granted in Yavnean rulings.

The fourth is that what is used for sitting or lying is susceptible to <u>midras</u> uncleanness. What is not used for sitting or lying is susceptible to corpse -- and other uncleanness. The cases are at M. 26:5D-F and M. 28:2.

The fifth and final principle is that a damaged clay utensil in the tent of a corpse does not afford protection. Eliezer's view, that we do partition clay utensils (M. 8:6, against the sages of M. 8:1) is probably new to him; the sages, I think, carry forward an inherited rule, or, rather, affirm an inherited anomaly.

Let us now contrast the established principles with those which seem to have been created to begin with in the Yavnean period. These raise quite fundamental issues.

A. How to render an oven susceptible to uncleanness or insusceptible?

1. M. 5:10A-C + 5:8C: If one cut an oven into rings and removed the plaster, it is clean. Eliezer says it is not clean.
2. M. 5:1/4:4E: Making an oven susceptible to uncleanness is a dispute between Judah and Meir, based upon a disagreement between Eliezer and Aqiba. It is difficult to see that the issue had been raised and settled before Eliezer and Aqiba, whose argument is wholly exegetical and cites no antecedent rules or precedents, let alone established cases.

B. Does an inverted, sealed jar afford protection in the tent of a corpse?

1. M. 10:1: Eliezer's view and that of the sages shows no principle common to both opinions.

C. The meaning of connection

1. M. 23:1 does not suggest than an established, antecedent opinion was available to both parties.
2. T. B.Q. 3:4 likewise does not appear to have been based upon an established principle about connecting patch to wood, or even about how connections were to be effected.
3. M. 28:7, by contrast, affirms for all parties that a patch must be firmly attached to form a connector.

To the degree that the principle of connection was taken for granted at Yavneh and may have derived from pre-70 times, it consisted solely of the proposition that objects connected to one another in a very firm way would convey uncleanness to one another. The modes of purification of connected objects, by contrast, cannot have been raised before Ushan times.

D. Whole Utensils and Broken Utensils

While it is clear that all Yavneans took for granted a broken utensil was clean, the issue is raised by Eliezer and Joshua about whether susceptibility and purification applies also to broken ones.

1. M. 14:7 + M. 18:9: Eliezer holds susceptibility and purification pertain only to whole utensils. Joshua says sherds are also subject to uncleanness. I do not see how the antecedent law can have raised the questions.
2. M. 17:1: The size of a perforation which renders a utensil insusceptible.

E. The Beginning and End of Susceptibility

1. The question of unfinished metal utensils and whether they are susceptible seems first raised by Gamaliel + Aqiba (M. 14:1, 14:5). + M. 12:6.

2. M. 28:2: Is throwing out a cloth an act of purification? Is discarding equivalent to breaking?

While it may be reasonable to suppose that from pre-70 times came rulings on the susceptibility of numerous specific objects in point of fact we are unable to find a Yavnean attestation for major lists of such objects. The Yavnean discussions of individual items, it already is clear, involve just a few general principles, in the main, about the autonomy and distinctiveness of a utensil. So it cannot be shown that in the tradition before 70 were rulings on many individual items, from which general principles were deduced. On the whole, the contrary seems to have been the pattern. This is an unexpected -- if very tentative -- result.

It generally is supposed both that the Houses go back to the time of Shammai and Hillel, ca. A.D. 10, and that their traditions attest the state of the law in at least the last fifty years before 70. But this cannot be taken for granted, for the names of the Houses are routinely used as mnemonic devices for the recording of opinions on controverted matters. Ushans, for example, do not hesitate to supply to the Houses a more complex problem, for their established opinions ("unclean," "clean') than is originally given. They will supply the Houses' names to disputes on principles first under discussion long after 70. We cannot, therefore, take for granted that the attributions to the Houses invariably supply firm evidence of the relative antiquity of sayings, for the criterion employed above, to show the relative reliability of attributions to Yavneans, then Ushans, does not apply without variation or exception. That is to say, while opinions attributed to Ushans, where relevant to matters covered in opinions attributed to Yavneans, nearly always in substance and reasoning follow upon Yavnean sayings, taking for granted and augmenting their conclusions, the same is not so for the Houses. Indeed, we observe in at least one instance, M. 18:1, that we have opinions on the same matter both in the names of the Houses, and in the names of Ushans in behalf of the Houses, and in the names of Ushans without reference to the Houses at all. The same matter, moreover, depends on a dispute between Meir and Judah in M. 15:1.

In order, therefore, to make use of the Houses' disputes in assessing the state of the law before 70, we have to reconsider each item and ask whether it seems to refer to Ushan issues and modes of inquiry or whether it seems ignorant of them. Only in the latter case will it be possible with some certainty to assign the substance of the Houses' opinion to the period of Yavneh or even earlier. For, obviously, if the Houses debated an issue, and the decided law was assigned to the Hillelites, then the Ushans should not have faced and worked on the same matter or principle. The cases, are as follows:

1. M. 9:2/M. 10:1: Does a tightly-fitting cover afford protection to a metal object or only food, liquid, and other clay objects?
2. M. 11:3: The susceptibility of nails. The context requires the issue to concern nails the origin of which we do not know. But by itself, the issue

is simply nails -- as with Sadoq, M. 12:4-5, with the criteria of autonomy and distinctiveness taken for granted.

3. M. 14:2E-H: Again, the context imposes a complex issue. But by itself, the Houses' dispute concerns when a siphon ceases to constitute a susceptible object. The principles at hand, on which all parties agree, are 1. autonomy and 2. usefulness. These assuredly are Yavnean at the latest. The Shammaites require damage, the Hillelites, attachment. It will naturally follow from the dispute that an object which is damaged or loses its independent status becomes insusceptible, and other disputes which take for granted the same principle will be equally authentic to Yavneh, if not earlier.

The Ushan attestation in T. B.M. 4:5 does not introduce new principles. It does, however, indicate that the two established ones may be assigned to either House. That means the Ushans had no tradition assigning usefulness as the primary criterion for one House, autonomy to the other (as with Judah/Meir materials) -- surely a sign of the authenticity of the dispute. But, as often, the Ushan redefinition of the issue hardly tells us what was the problem to begin with.

4. M. 20:2: The issue is whether the trough is used for sitting. The Hillelites say it is not, therefore it is susceptible only to corpse-uncleanness. The Shammaites say it is, so it is susceptible to midras. Accordingly, on the surface the Yavnean (and Scriptural) principle that that which is used for sitting is susceptible to midras is applied to an intermediate item. The remainder of M. 20:2 assumes the correctness of the Shammaite view. Here we cannot suppose Meir's stress on form (M. 19:9-10) is necessarily behind, or to be read into, the pericope. + T. B.M. 11:3.

5. M. 20:6: A sheet used for lying loses its susceptibility to midras when it is not longer available for lying. This takes place, all parties agree, when it is no longer a sheet but is turned into a curtain. The only issue is when that takes place. Aqiba participates in the structure, as well as the issue, of the pericope. But T. B.M. 1:8 ignores the Houses entirely. Yose b. R. Judah and Eleazar b. R. Simeon debate whether the sheet, after being made into a curtain, is susceptible at all. The Houses take for granted that it is susceptible. T. B.M. 11:8E assumes "purification" means complete insusceptibility, not merely from midras. + T. B.M. 11:9.

6. M. 22:4E-H: A chair affixed to a trough is susceptible to midras, the Shammaites say. It remains an autonomous object. The Hillelites say it is unsusceptible, having lost its identity. Shammai says even if it is carved into the trough, it is susceptible. I do not see how the Houses' dispute differs from M. 20:3. An unclean chair attached to a post is

unclean -- it retains its autonomy. One made on a post is unclean -- Shammai's position. Here again we have the Shammaites view without a dispute. M. 20:5 relates in the same way.

7. M. 26:6: The issue is whether the bag will be used for sitting.
8. M. 28:4: If "susceptible" means, to midras, then the issue is as above. The Shammaites hold the wrappers will be used for sitting. The Hillelites hold those which are ornamented will not be used for sitting. Gamaliel is internal to the structure of the pericope. Yose and Simeon attest. The reading of Simeon b. Gamaliel is difficult.
9. T. B.B. 5:7-8: A belt made out of the side of a garment needs no hem, the Shammaites hold. The Hillelites say it needs a hem. I am not sure what principle is at hand. Perhaps it comes down to whether the belt is an autonomous object without some hem. Ushans attest.
10. T. B.M. 4:16/M. 14:8: The principle taken for granted by both Houses is that a utensil to be susceptible must serve its normal purpose.

The disputes between the Houses which do not seem to concern problems unfamiliar at Yavneh at the latest thus take for granted the following principles:

1. The effects of a tight-fitting cover: No. 1.
2. A susceptible object is one which is a utensil, that is, autonomous and of distinctive character: Nos. 2, 3, 6, 9 (?), 10.
3. The difference between midras- and corpse-uncleanness is whether or not an object is used for sitting: Nos. 4, 5, 6, 7, 8.

We have, in addition, several items which seems to involve principles otherwise unattested for Yavneh, as follows:

1. M. 15:1: Judah and Meir debate the susceptibility of vessels which hold more than forty se'ahs etc. Meir says they are susceptible, Judah says they are not. Meir will not care when a utensil reaches the specified volume or how we know that volume. It makes no difference to him. Only to Judah is this a significant issue. Accordingly, the debate, M. 18:1, on how we measure a utensil's volume is important only to Judah and depends on his opinion. M. 18:1 is probably pseudepigraphic. The silence of Yavneans on the question probably means it is Ushan to begin with. Underlying Judah's and Meir's dispute is the issue of form (Meir) vs. function (Judah), and that same issue may be discerned in M. 14:2 (use vs. autonomy). So it is possible, but I think highly improbable, that both Houses' regarded use as primary consideration, and so, early and independently, came to the second-level issue debated here. Overall, however, I think the version of M. 18:1 is pseudepigraphic. M. 18:1 is

attested by Yose who shares Judah's view of the centrality of function, and Simeon Shezuri, whose opinion on the larger issue we do not know.

2. M. 22:4A-D: The houses debate the susceptibility of a bride's chair which cannot be used for a bride. The Shammaites hold it is still susceptible as a container. The Hillelites say it is clean. Here the issue can only be secondary purpose, with the Shammaites in accord with Meir's view in M. 19:9-10.
3. M. 29:8: The length of various remnants. We do not have a single Yavnean ruling on this matter. The mnemonic purpose is self-evident; Yose gloss marks it as Ushan at the latest. Perhaps it also is an Ushan mnemonic.
4. T. B.M. 3:8: Nathan b. R. Joseph assigns Meir's principle to the House of Shammai.

[5. T. B.Q. 6:18: Eleazar b. R. Simeon phrases as a Houses' dispute M. 9:6's rule that new peat may be clean. But old peat may not be unclean. M. is not relevant to Kelim, and I do not know what principle is at hand.]

Of these items, No. 1 is the most likely to represent pseudepigraphic use of the names of the Houses for mnemonic purposes. It looks as though the names of the Houses are used either in support of Judah's position, with both Houses agreeing with him, as in No. 1, or in contradiction to Meir's, with Meir represented as Shammaite, hence rejected, as in Nos. 2 and 4. The mnemonic value of the Houses names to preserve the sequence, seven through ten, is obvious in M. 29:8, but the primary reason for supposing that the item is Ushan is the otherwise unknown issue of the pericope, the lengths of remnants. Without a single Yavnean allusion to that matter, we can hardly suppose the item to be accurately attributed to the pre-Yavnean Houses. No. 5 is difficult only because it is not a problem of Kelim, so we cannot assess the state of Yavnean opinion on it.

We thus are on firm grounds to assign to the period before 70 three very fundamental issues.

First is an effort to work out the effects of a tightly-fitting cover on clay utensils in the tent of a corpse, with the problem of deciding the result of such a cover for metal.

Second, on the definition of a utensil, all parties are in agreement that an object constitutes a utensil and is susceptible when it is autonomous and exhibits distinctive character and use.

Finally comes the view that midras-uncleanness affects things used for sitting, with the concommitant principle that when something formerly employed for that purpose ceases to be useful it ceases to be susceptible to midras uncleanness.

When we review the principles clearly assigned to Yavnean authorities, we find these same three principles or issues, and in addition, the matter of the division of utensils, receptacles, breakage as purification, the relationship of metal to wood. Of these items, only the last two look to be important innovations of the Yavnean thinkers, for the division of utensils and the closely-related matter of the division of utensils are issues attributed to the time of Gamaliel the Elder and, in the latter instance, Yohanan b. Zakkai. Both are contemporaries of the Houses.

Let us now consider the relationships between these principles and their Scriptural foundations, to see which of them is apt to have required an extensive antecedent exegetical tradition or indeed to have been generated by exegesis of Scripture at all.

iii. From Mishnah To Scripture

Two issues are before us. First, to what degree are the several earliest laws or principles based upon the plain meaning of Scriptures? Second, in what measure do the statements of principles either presuppose or make explicit a considerable, antecedent exegesis of Scriptures? For example, if a Yavnean law is worked out primarily through reasoning, without reference to Scriptural support, then we may hardly imagine that an ancient exegetical tradition, long under development, stands behind the result of the reasoning or, indeed, that the sages had in hand any sort of tradition of all.

Let us now review those Scriptures pertinent to the laws of utensils, observing also the Scriptures which seem to have generated no laws at all. The relevant passages are as follows:

> Lev. 11:29: And these are unclean to you among the swarming things that swarm upon the earth...
>
> 11:31: These [afore-named] are unclean to you among all that swarm. Whoever touches them when they are dead shall be unclean until the evening.
>
> 11:32: And anything upon which any of them falls when they are dead shall be unclean, whether it is an article of wood or a garment or a skin or a sack, any vessel that is used for any purpose; it must be put into water, and it shall be unclean until the evening. Then it shall be clean.
>
> 11:33: And if any of them falls into any earthen vessel, all that is in it shall be unclean, and you shall break it.
>
> 11:34: Any food in it which may be eaten, upon which water may come, shall be unclean; and all drink which may be drunk from every such vessel shall be unclean.
>
> 11:35: And everything upon which any part of their carcass falls shall be unclean; whether oven or stove, it shall be broken in pieces; they are unclean, and shall be unclean to you.
>
> Lev. 15:4-6: Every bed on which he who has the discharge lies shall be unclean; and everything on which he sits shall be unclean. And any one who touches his bed shall wash his clothes and bathe himself in water, and be unclean until the evening. And whoever sits on anything on which he who has the discharge has sat shall wash his clothes and bathe himself in water and be unclean until the evening.
>
> Lev. 15:9-12: And any saddle on which he who has the discharge rides shall be unclean. And whoever touches anything that was under him shall be

unclean until the evening; and he who carries such a thing shall wash his clothes and bathe himself in water and be unclean until the evening. Any one whom he that has the discharge touches without having rinsed his hands in water shall wash his clothes and bathe himself in water and be unclean until the evening.

Lev. 15:19-24: When a woman has a discharge of blood which is her regular discharge from her body, she shall be in her impurity for seven days, and whoever touches her shall be unclean until the evening. And everything upon which she lies during her impurity shall be unclean; everything also upon which she sits shall be unclean. And whoever touches her bed shall wash his clothes and bathe himself in water and be unclean until the evening. And whoever touches anything upon which she sits shall wash his clothes and bathe himself in water and be unclean until the evening, whether it is the bed or anything upon which she sits, when he touches it he shall be unclean until the evening.

Num. 19:14-15: This is the law when a man dies in a tent: everyone who comes into the tent, and everyone who is in the tent, shall be unclean seven days. And every open vessel, which has no cover fastened upon it, is unclean.

Num. 31:19-24: Encamp outside the camp seven days; whoever of you has killed any person, and whoever has touched any slain, purify yourselves and your captives on the third day and on the seventh day. You shall purify every garment, every article of skin, all work of goats' hair, and every article of wood. And Eleazar the priest said to the men of war who had gone to battle: This is the statute of the law which the Lord has commanded Moses: Only the gold, the silver, the bronze, the iron, the tin, and the lead, everything that can stand the fire, you shall pass through the fire and it shall be clean. Nevertheless it shall also be purified with the water of impurity; and whatever cannot stand the fire you shall pass through the water. You must wash your clothes on the seventh day, and you shall be clean; and afterward you shall come into the camp.

Without further ado, we may eliminate from further consideration three Yavnean or pre-Yavnean principles.

1. Midras-uncleanness affects something which is used for sitting or lying.

This matter is made explicit in Lev. 15:4-6, 9-12, and 19-24. No one had to look further than these verses to find the view that things used for sitting are susceptible to midras-uncleanness. This applies both for sitting (moshav) and for riding (merkav), as we saw. What lies behind the concept of pressure, or midras, however, is not to be gainsaid; but it is not, at present, our problem.

2. The effects of the tent over the corpse-uncleanness are nullified by a tightly-sealed cover.

Num. 19:15 is simply turned into an affirmative statement. Every closed vessel, with a tightly-sealed cover, is clean. The Houses' debate (M. 9:2) on clay utensils' protection for metal is phrased entirely in terms of rational analysis, without a hint as to an antecedent tradition based on Scriptural exegesis.

The proper location of the cover seems also to be a point first raised by Eliezer.

3. Breaking a clay utensil cleans it.

Lev. 11:33 is simply completed: All that is in it shall be unclean, and you shall break it and then it is clean. All issues on breaking as purification depend upon that simple allegation. All are Yavnean or later, based on rational inquiry into the meaning of breaking, investigated in accord with the principle that a susceptible object is one which is useful -- a utensil. So breaking means rendering useless. It goes without saying that, since Scripture is clear, no one will have had to engage in elaborate processes of reasoning or argument to conclude that a perforated or broken -- thus useless -- utensil is insusceptible.

The central issue of utensils, however, concerns normal use, distinctiveness, autonomy, and the whole range of conceptions intimately related to use. Without finding that fundamental conception in Scriptures, we shall have to look for, or at least postulate, a very substantial layer of exegesis, conceptual innovation, or both. How would a legal philosopher, whenever he lived, have come to the conception that a random object becomes a utensil, therefore is susceptible, at the point at which it is useful, and ceases to be a utensil, therefore becomes insusceptible, when it is useless?

It seems to me the answer is simply that, opening Scripture, anyone at any time will have found the following at Lev. 11:32: "Any vessel that is used for any purpose," KL KLY 'SR Y^{C}SH ML'KH BHM. The point is that, since there are some objects, also referred to as KLY, which are not "used for any purpose," after listing various materials, Scripture adds, "every utensil." This must function as an inclusionary phrase, followed by "used for any purpose," a limiting one -- and the rest follows. That very simple process of reasoning, governing the answer to the question, raised throughout our study, "when is a KLY a utensil?" begins in a not very close reading of Scripture. So much for an object as utensil, that is, as something useful.

Now let us ask about autonomy and distinctiveness. These, I think, are the clear intent of the construction in inclusionary, then exclusionary, clauses: "Every KLY made of any material" will include any object whatsoever. Then, "any KLY used for any purpose" excludes the just-stated proposition, for we no longer have in mind any KLY, meaning any object, but now refer explicitly to any KYL meaning any useful object. In other words, as soon as we refer to use, autonomy and distinctiveness will, in the nature of Scripture, follow in its wake. Indeed, it is entirely possible that the categories of autonomy and distinctiveness ("having a name of its own") are Mishnaic ways of rephrasing the primary Scriptural statement, "with which work is done."

Add to this the view that an insusceptible utensil is one which is broken, and the matter of usefulness is reenforced. Restatements of the same matter will include the issue of permanence, on the one side, or perforation and breaking on the other. In this matter we then include the oven. Everyone will agree breaking an oven purifies it, since Lev. 11:33 says so. The only question is, What is breaking? The conception of Eliezer in M. 5:10A is that breaking the oven and then reconstructing it so that it is useful, but not in its former form, does not constitute breaking. So Eliezer's notion, carried forward by Judah, is that "breaking" means "rendering useless," with stress on function, and not merely altering the primary form. If the oven still functions as before, despite the alteration of its form, it will be susceptible. What is important in this instance is the primary and unmediated resort to Scripture, the spelling out of matters directly consequent upon the open-endedness of the Scriptural statement.

Let us now ask about the matter of receptacles and the closely-related issue of the division of a utensil into inner and outer parts. Lev. 11:33 speaks of "falling into its midst" ('L TWKW), with the exegetical result: "That which has a 'midst'" against that which does not. Clearly, the interpretation of TWK to mean "that which has an inside, a receptacle," is not going to require a great many intervening stages of reasoning. Once we are told "whatever falls into the midst," it is going to be a short step indeed to a negative formulation, "what has no 'midst'" is not going to be subject to the susceptibility of an insect in contained air space. So far we are in close accord with the simple meaning of the verse.

The saying of Hezekiah before Gamaliel the Elder, and the conception attested to, but hardly originated by, Yohanan b. Zakkai that which has a receptacle is susceptible, simply make explicit what Scripture makes quite clear to begin with. There is, however, an important qualification. Lev. 11:33 speaks of clay utensils, and so too does Hezekiah. Yet by the time of the saying attributed to Yohanan b. Zakkai, "the midst" of a clay utensil has been extended to all utensils. And this is central to the interpretation of Yohanan b. Zakkai's materials in M. 17:16, therefore to M. 17:15 as well: Whatever has a receptacle -- <u>of any sort</u> -- is susceptible. The key words must therefore be MKL MQWM, of any sort, with the qualification as to permanence and use of secondary importance. The distance from "TWK of clay utensils" to TWK of any sort of utensil has been covered, so to speak, from Gamaliel the Elder to Yohanan b. Zakkai, who comments on a secondary effect of the larger rule, concerning all receptacles.

I tend to think that some time between the point of Hezekiah's testimony -- let us say, ca. 40 A.D. -- and the observation of Yohanan b. Zakkai -- let us say, 75 A.D. (to speak in unrefined terms for the moment, for Yohanan, after all, was a contemporary of Gamaliel the Elder), the conception of receptacle was applied to all sorts of utensils made of all sorts of materials. Obviously, this sort of guess relies upon many infirm presuppositions, first, about the accuracy of attributions, also about the correctness of our interpretation of the meaning of the two sayings. But, assuming for the moment we are right, what will have taken place between Gamaliel the Elder and Yohanan b. Zakkai?

I think all that has happened is a reading of Lev. 11:33 in the context of 11:32. Lev. 11:32 speaks of objects made of any material, limited by the insistence that they be useful. Lev. 11:33 then speaks specifically of any earthen vessel, but its point is not that the vessel has to have 'an inside' -- that is Hezekiah's point. Lev. 11:33 simply states that if a creeping thing falls into any earthen vessel, the vessel's contents will be susceptible. All the exegete has to have done is take at face value the reference to the "inside," at the same time correctly interpreting that reference to be tangential to the point of the law. That is, the law does not state, "clay utensils alone have an inner part," which is contaminable through its airspace (the falling of the creeping thing into the contained space). The Scripture takes for granted there is a contained space, explaining the effects of a creeping thing's falling into it. The exegete then will have taken for granted that anything which in like manner forms a receptacle is going to be susceptible. What Lev. 11:33 will have told him is that only clay utensils' airspace is susceptible, excluding the airspace of utensils made of other materials.

Two important ideas have been ignored, first, the division of utensils, second, the relationship of wood to metal. I am unable to see any basis in Scripture for that latter issue, let alone for the way in which it is resolved. If, as I suppose, it is a Yavnean contribution, then it stands to reason it is a point raised at Yavneh specifically because settled issues involving utility and serviceability raised secondary ones, concerning the primary surface which is used. I tend to think the conception of wood as secondary and of metal as primary simply is based upon the recognition of the primary function of the metal object attached to a wood handle. The specific problem, for example, the spinner adjudged by Aqiba (either susceptible or insusceptible, depending on the tradition we prefer), hardly seems important. It is the Ushans who showed the conceptual profundity of the issue. Joshua's simple observation that he cannot explain the inherited ruling certainly shows, I think, that some sort of rules came down to Yavneh on the subject: Joshua cannot fully explain the anomalies. In this minor matter, the relationship to Scripture cannot have been clear to Joshua, and the probable reason is that there was none.

The saying of Hezekiah to Gamaliel the Elder marks the earliest phase in the formation of an exegetical tradition on the matter of the cleanness of utensils. When, as shown here, we separate the exegeses from the attached citations of M., we find pretty much the same principles attested at Yavneh or by the Houses: first, usefulness is decisive, with the further point, perhaps Yavnean, that usefulness is determined by human needs; second, utensils may be divided and subdivided; third, breaking ("overturning") purifies ovens. Nothing generated by exegesis is apt to reflect issues or principles important at some unknown time before the last decades of the Temple's existence and the first years of Yavneh. Over all, it is very difficult to suppose that the fundamental issues and principles which underlie the development of Kelim depend upon an exegetical tradition beginning at any point before the first century. To be sure, anyone might have opened Scriptures and learned that an object forms a susceptible utensil when it is used for some work -- that is, when it is useful. But if that obvious conclusion was drawn, it produced no result whatsoever before the mid-first century at the earliest. The same is so of the other exegeses of Scripture pertinent to the earliest parts of the laws of Kelim.

iv. Conclusion

The Yavnean rulings were based upon a number of important, presupposed principles, which were apt to derive from the period before 70. The most important part of these was that an object which is useful is susceptible, and one which is useless is not. In like manner, it was a given for Yavneans that a broken utensil is insusceptible, merely a corollary of the former.

The second principle, directly attributed to authorities before 70, was that a clay utensil without an inner part has no outer parts; this is either restated by, or itself generates, the further data of Yavnean law, first, that a utensil with a receptacle is susceptible, and one without is not, and second, that utensils are divided, for the purpose of assessing their status as to uncleanness, into inner and outer parts.

Two further principles, assuredly pre-70, were, first, that what is used for sitting or lying is susceptible to midras-uncleanness, other things being susceptible only to corpse-uncleanness; and, second, that a partitioned clay utensil in the corpse's tent affords protection. All of these rules, we have seen, derive directly from the plain meaning of Scripture; no extensive intervening exegetical tradition can be located. In Chapter Ten, Zabim, I reconstruct that tradition.

Some of these principles were taken for granted in rulings evidently reliably attributed to the Houses. That means that the materials taken for granted at Yavneh very likely go back at least for about half-a-century before that time. The principles involve a tightly fitting cover, the susceptibility of useful, and the insusceptibility of useless, objects, the susceptibility to midras of something used for sitting, and the insusceptibility to midras of something not used for sitting (or lying). All three principles derive directly from Scripture; none, it hardly needs repeating, rests upon a considerable exegetical tradition. If the attributions to the Houses are authentic and if the Houses formed historical entities dating from the early decades of the first century, then these three matters will have marked the beginning of the laws of Kelim.

We have found no evidence, therefore, that Kelim rests upon four or five hundred years of antecedent Scriptural exegesis. We have, indeed, found remarkably little evidence of an intensive development of the law from the Houses to Yavneh through either Scriptural exegesis or through reasoning. If the state of the earliest law is accurately represented by the Houses, then it seems not unreasonable to suggest that the matter of Kelim began with them or with their masters. From that point the main lines of legal development before 70 probably involved the matters represented by Hezekiah's saying, on the one side, and by Eliezer's dispute in M. 8:1, on the other. That is, the direction of legal development was in terms of dividing utensils -- for both matters come back to the effects of doing just that. Obviously, the principle that a susceptible object is one which is useful could have led to a great many specific rulings, and perhaps it did, but we cannot demonstrate it. What I think more likely is that the first fifty years of legal development, from ca. 20 to ca. 70, were marked by the laying forth of the most fundamental points on usefulness, on the one side, and division, on the other, in addition to the simplest issues of the status of a utensil in the tent of a corpse.

Our firm result is that the laws of Kelim could have begun their development at any point, from the redaction of Leviticus onward, at which someone opened the pertinent verses of Scripture and decided to apply them to utensils not involved in the cult, part of a larger intention to keep purity laws outside the Temple. No considerable exegesis was then required to demonstrate that the Torah required pretty much what the authorities before 70 and immediately afterward took at face value. While, as I said, the laws of Kelim could have begun their development any time from the completion of Leviticus to the first century, the greatest probability is that the laws of Kelim began their development shortly before the Houses. It is only then, as we saw, that the traces of a secondary exegetical tradition are to be found, resting on something more complex than the simple and plain meaning of the Scriptures themselves. It was then that the most fundamental and original conception of all took shape: utensils not in the Temple and not used for the cult to begin with should be subject to uncleanness. That, after all, is what is taken for granted even by the Houses' rulings. And neither Scriptures nor exegesis of Scriptures will have generated such an original and revolutionary conception. The mere passage of time accounts for nothing. I think it likely that some one person or a small group of people effected the most profound development of all, laying the foundations for our tractate.

CHAPTER THREE
OHALOT

i. Unattributed Sayings

I can locate in Ohalot only fourteen pericopae which contain no clear signs of attribution or attestation. Of these, however, six, signified by brackets, seem to belong to an isolable and identifiable stratum, or at the very least, to be taken for granted at a particular time. In addition, Nos. 4 (unimportant), and 11 (important) seem to belong to a particular stratum, in both instances, to Usha. Interest in connection (No. 5) is predominantly Ushan. But the evidence does not warrant placing these items in parentheses. If Ohalot contains laws deriving from the period before 70, and if those laws are signified by not being marked by attribution or reference to particular, named authorities, then those laws do not survive in any significant quantity. True, they would have been, and probably are, subsumed in named sayings. But that is a separate problem. The conception that unnamed sayings, because they are unnamed, may be assumed to come from the period before 70 is, for Ohalot, false. On the contrary, if we were forced to take a guess, then we should probably be wise to suppose the absence of an attribution signifies a later, not an earlier, tradition -- an Ushan, not a Yavnean item. For materials lacking an attribution very commonly take for granted not only the thematic agendum of Usha, but also its particular problems and theories. Further, a considerable number of unattributed sentences derive from Tosefta. It would be exceedingly difficult to show that that material was formulated in the version now before us before 70 (or much afterward). On the contrary, the evidence we do have -- unattributed declarative sentences -- suggest we are in the middle of Usha, not in the period before 70 or in Yavnean circles.

1. M. 1:6: A man does not convey uncleanness until he dies (+ T. 2:1).
2. T. 1:4: Gentile, beast, etc. which touch corpse -- utensils which touch them are clean, etc.
3. T. 1:5: Marrow is unclean.
4. T. 1:6: Gloss of M.

[5. M. 3:3F-G, M. 3:4: Whatever pertains to corpse is unclean... Connection effected by man is no connection. Not clearly attested, but probably Ushan at latest, as in T. 4:8: Jacob takes rule for granted.]

[6. T. 4:9: All corpse-excretions are clean. Setting is Ushan.]

[7. T. 4:12: There are three kinds of quarter-logs. Certainly Ushan.]

[8. M. 3:7/T. 5:3: A cubic handbreadth introduces the uncleanness and interposes ... + Apocopated examples. No clear attestation. But T. 7:4 shows Simeon takes it for granted.]

[9. M. 9:16/T. 10:9, 10, 11: This set does not contain a single attribution. Yet it is in form closely parallel to 9:1-14, which are probably Ushan, and to 10:1-3, which certainly are Ushan. M. 9:16 forms a bridge between the two chapters.]

10. T. 11:9: Jar of purification-water hung in hatchway. M. 10:1-3 surely are Ushan, but this case is separate from their problem.

11. M. 10:4-6, T. 11:11. 1-5: No attributions or attestations help with this important composite. But the indications of M. 10:1-3, are strong that we have an Ushan problem throughout.

12. M. 12:4/T. 13:4, 5A: Sandal of cradle. Illustrate M. 1:1-3, which are Yavnean.

[13. M. 12:5/T. 13:7, 8, 9: Yose glosses the rule on the column, thus the whole set has a terminus at Usha.]

[14. T. 16:9: Three kinds of graves. But the pattern of M. 18:2-4, which is Ushan, predominates.]

As I said, it is difficult to locate much of an "unattributed corpus of law," and virtually impossible to find in what we do have any evidence of origin before 70. I am inclined to see only Nos. 1, 2, 3, 4, 11, and possibly 12 as entirely without evidence as to a particular provenance. Of these, No. 12 is most likely to belong in the same stratum as M. 1:1-3. Nos. 1-3 are important. No. 11 is important, because these are significant rules, carefully worked out. I should be surprised if the set is not Ushan, simply because the conceptions and modes of thought in No. 11 are distinctive to the Ushan circles, and because we cannot find in Yavneh a hint at interest in these same conceptions or at the presence of such modes of thought. That is not a decisive argument: the item under discussion may itself be adduced as evidence for Yavneh as readily as for Usha, in the absence of other evidence. But for Usha we do have evidence, which is, after all, in the very same redactional structure.

ii. Ohalot before 70

Let us turn to the presuppositons of the Houses and Yavneans, those points agreed upon by all parties, or, of still greater probative value, taken for granted by all parties without the need of articulate agreement at all. They should allow us accurately to describe the heritage of rules, principles, and fundamental conceptions going back to the period before 70 and before the Houses, to whom, for convenience sake, we may assign a date of 40-50. These presuppositions seem to have been the following.

I. Houses

Modes

1. A Tent spreads contamination when it overshadows a corpse (M. 2:3) or the excretions or remains of a corpse (M. 2:1). A corpse and things like a corpse contaminate in a Tent.

Sources

2. A grave-area is assumed to contain corpse-matter (which may be removed). (M. 16:4. 5, 18:1, 18:4).
3. A dwelling of a gentile in the Land of Israel is unclean (M. 18:7).

Tents

4. The standard measure is a handbreadth (M. 3:6, M. 15:1-3, 11:1-3).
5. If one door is open by a handbreadth, the uncleanness will exude from that door, so what is subject to other doors is now unaffected (M. 7:3). The same principle is in M. 11:1-2.
6. Compressed uncleanness is that in a space of less than requisite size. It spurts up and down, but is not spread to the sides (M. 15:3).
[7. Holes give passage to uncleanness if they are adequate to their own purpose (M. 13:1-2).]
8. A Tent consists of an enclosed, empty space of a cubic handbreadth (M. 11:3-7). = No. 4.
9. Diminishing the space open in a hatchway by means of a pot prevents the passage of corpse-uncleanness (M. 5:1-4). The suppositions are (1) corpse-uncleanness passes through a handbreadth and through no lesser space; (2) the pot does diminish, so interposes. The principle of conjoining with the walls of the Tent is assumed by the Houses in M. 11:8. + T. for M. 15:9.

II. Yavneans

Modes

10. A human being who touches a corpse becomes unclean for seven days. A utensil becomes unclean in the same degree as the corpse itself (M. 1:1-3, M. 15:10).
11. Movables contaminate by overshadowing if they are a handbreadth in size. (M. 15:10, 16:1-2). The standard measure of a Tent applies to movables.
12. Blood contaminates (M. 2:2).
13. Dirt from a grave-area and dirt from abroad contaminate (M. 17:5).

Sources

14. Limbs and other parts of the body contaminate (T. 2:7-8).
15. Things which have exuded from a corpse contaminate (M. 2:2. 3:5).
16. Things connected with the grave (stones) contaminate (M. 2:4. 16:3).
17. Dirt which may contain bone matter contaminates (M. 17:2).

Tents

18. Utensils afford protection along with walls of Tents (M. 5:5-6).

If we now further reduce these presuppositions to the simplest and most comprehensive propositions, what do we have?

1. Tents spread contamination produced by corpses and things similar to corpses (1, 2, 10, 13, 14, 15, 16, 17). It is particularly striking that the several Yavnean preconceptions here stand close to, but develop in some small way, the givens of the Houses' rulings.

2. Gentiles' land and dwellings in the Land of Israel are unclean (3,13). This is not an important aspect of Ohalot.

3. A Tent is a handbreadth in surface area (whether or not we require sides, doors, etc.) (4,8). The point is that corpse-uncleanness requires a space of a handbreadth for its passage. If, therefore, we have egress of a handbreadth, corpse-uncleanness will exude. If we have a cover or protection on the upper surface of a handbreadth, corpse-uncleanness will not descend into the covered area (7, 8, 9 + 5).

4. Corpse-matter in a space less than a handbreadth in cubic measure is regarded as compressed. It spurts upward and downward, but is not spread to the sides, since we do not have a Tent to accomplish the spreading (6).

5. The converse of No. 4 is that corpse-matter in a space of a handbreadth which lacks adequate egress (a handbreadth) is regarded as in a sealed tomb, contaminating on all sides. The point is that here we do have a Tent to spread the uncleanness, but we do not have a door to release it. All parts of the enclosed space are going to produce contamination, on the one hand, but we do not have interposition, on the part of the Tent, on the other (No. 5).

6. Space for the transfer of corpse-uncleanness is adequate if that space serves some useful and intended purpose (No. 7, contradicts Nos. 4, 5, 6, 8, 9).

To come to a still simpler formulation: Corpses contaminate and Tents interpose. Tents are made up by surfaces of a handbreadth's width, breadth and height.

iii. From Mishnah to Scripture

The first important principle of Ohalot is that corpses contaminate for seven days, and this, of course, comes to us from Num. 19:11: "He who touches the dead body of any person shall be unclean for seven days." The same verse, moreover, tells us that corpse-contamination is conveyed through contact (touching). The person who touches the corpse is unclean with the seven days, or corpse-uncleanness. Contamination by the mode, or means, of a Tent is declared in Num. 19:14: "This is the law when a man dies in a tent: every one who comes into the tent, and every one who is in the tent, shall be unclean seven days." The tent thus (so to speak) serves as a Tent, that is, whatever is overshadowed by the tent is made unclean through overshadowing, the Tent's affect, which is to spread the corpse uncleanness to all beneath its shadow, as if the person in the tent has touched the corpse itself.

What about utensils in the Tent? Num. 19:15 says, "And every open vessel, which has no cover fastened upon it, is unclean." The contrary is that every closed and sealed vessel is clean. That can mean only, the contents of the vessel, not the outer surface.

Num. 19:16 intends to tell us about a corpse not in a Tent, "Whoever in the open field touches one who is slain with a sword or a dead body or a bone of a man or a grave shall be unclean seven days." One would not have to be a very clever exegete to learn from this verse that things which are like the corpse or grave -- the bone, the grave-area itself -- produce corpse-contamination. Further, we learn that touching out of doors is equivalent to overshadowing in or by the Tent.

What about touching a utensil affected by a corpse? Num. 19:22 states, "But whatever the unclean person touches shall be unclean and any one who touches it shall be unclean until evening." This verse surely meant in the first place that whatever object the person unclean with corpse-uncleanness touches will be unclean in the same way as the person who has touched it. The converse -- the rule about someone who touches that unclean object -- is clearly stated. But outside of our opening chapter, M. 1:1-3, this matter is of no interest to Ohalot.

Now if we ask, Upon what foundation do the opening and closing parts of Ohalot, that is, the discussion of modes and sources of uncleanness, stand? the answer is very clear: Scripture, "the Written Torah," supplied with remarkably little exegesis, gives the laws pretty much as Mishnah -- "the Oral Torah" -- presents them. To return to the presuppositions of modes and sources of uncleanness, Nos. 1, 2, 10, 12, 13, 14, 15, 16, 17, all may be readily discerned as the implications of Scripture itself. The sole item which clearly is not based upon the Pentateuchal law is No. 3. So it is difficult to see the materials in M. 1:1-3:5 and 16:3-18:10 as much more than useful supplements to what Scripture makes clear.

What about Tents -- M. 3:6-16:2? When we pass the presupposition that Tents spread corpse-contamination, we have left the Scriptural domain entirely. Not a single concept or presupposition before us seems to derive directly or indirectly from the exegesis of Scripture.

If we now return to the most profound presuppositions of our tractate, we find the following: (1) a Tent requires egress. This, logically and concommitantly, links to (2) the sealed tomb. But that presupposition should not obscure the conception upon which these statements, in their turn, depend. Corpse-uncleanness passes through a handbreadth of open space. Its passage may be prevented, therefore, by a handbreadth of closed space. In other words, our entire tractate is founded upon a single conception, to which we refer, for the sake of convenience, as the standard measure.

And what imposes that "measure" is the trait of corpse-uncleanness. Everything else in one way or another is logically spun out of that single, fundamental trait of that which exudes from the corpse.

In no way is that concept related to Scripture. No exegete even tried to find some Scriptural foundation for it. And, as we recognize, what is at issue is not merely the measurement of a handbreadth, but all which is expressed by that simple measurement.

For what the "handbreadth in breadth, depth, and height" means is that the Scriptural tent, a place where people live, obviously has been left far behind us. The Tent of the tractate before us is anything but a place in which people dwell.

Now to spell this out: when we say a Tent must measure a handbreadth, either to prevent uncleanness from entering its enclosed space, or to keep uncleanness within its enclosed space (without regard to the nature of the enclosure -- walls or no walls), what is the meaning of such an allegation? What is this Tent to which reference is made in Ohalot? (Even if we substitute house for Tent, when house is used in Ohalot, the referent at some points seems to be burial niche, kokh, as much as a real house.) And what is it that can be contained in the Tent of which Ohalot speaks? The answer is not the body, for a whole body by definition is four times larger than a handbreadth, and therefore a body cannot be contained in a Tent. The terms of the answer, moreover, have to include that invisible viscous gas which is uncleanness, because it is everywhere taken for granted that uncleanness cannot penetrate a closed area of a handbreadth or less, on the one hand, or will be prevented from exuding by that same closed area, if it is enclosed by it.

Corpse-uncleanness is something which can be contained by a Tent. A Tent is something which can contain or interpose against corpse-uncleanness.

The one has -- in the nature of things -- to be defined in terms of the other. Our definition of a Tent is curiously out of phase with the simple meaning of Scripture. The issue of Scripture is drastically revised, indeed, when Tent becomes "that which can contain what exudes from a corpse." When, therefore, we define Tent as we do here, and as is taken for granted throughout the Mishnaic laws which depend upon the simple definition before us, we mean something entirely different from what Scripture means.

If the conception of death is that at death something leaves, exudes from, the body, then the Tent serves as the functional equivalent to the body, for it is able to receive and contain that which exudes from the body. The Tent, therefore, takes the place of the body, makes a place for that which, in the body, leaves at the point or moment of death. The Tent is to be understood as a surrogate for the body, restoring the order which has broken with the leaving of the body by that which exudes from it. Death has released this effusion. The Tent then contains it. We have avoided naming this thing which "exudes from the corpse at such a viscosity as to pass through an open space of a handbreadth or more, but no less." I see no point in calling it the soul and to allege that the "uncleanness" of the corpse is the "soul" which is the "spirit" surviving after death and requiring a new locale. But Philo seems to have had just a notion:

> Further, too, those who enter a house in which anyone has died are ordered not to touch anything until they have bathed themselves and also washed the clothes which they were wearing. And all the vessels and articles of furniture, and anything else that happens to be inside, practically everything is held by him to be unclean. For a man's soul is a precious thing, and when it departs to seek another home, all that will be left behind is defiled, deprived as it is of the divine image. For it is the mind of man which has the form of God, being shaped in conformity with the ideal archetype, the Word that is above all.
>
> Special Laws 3:206-207 (Trans. F.H. Colson, p. 605)

So while we went in search of a bridge to Scripture, provided by information contained in unattributed sayings in Mishnah-tractate Ohalot, we find ourselves at the end on the road to Alexandria. Where the framers of the generative proposition of Ohalot and Philo came across their idea of the character and fate of the soul after death we do not know. We may be sure, however, that if they looked in Scripture, they came up empty-handed. So the tractate at hand rests upon foundations other than in Scripture, and the unattributed sayings of the tractate, for their part, in no way lay forth the boundaries of these foundations.

CHAPTER FOUR
NEGAIM

i. Unattributed Sayings

Items in brackets are included for the sake of completeness. In fact, those items are susceptible of location in known strata, for reasons specified throughout. The reason for probable assignment of each such item is explained. This catalogue covers Sifra to Negaim and Mesora (SN, SM) as well.

[1. M. 1:3: Colors join together to clear, shut up, certify. M. 1:3 continues M. 1:1, which is suitably attested to Usha at M. 1:1C-D and to Yavneh at M. 1:2. The process of joining together of different shades is thus a secondary development of the recognition of the four distinct shades. + T. 1:3B: Spreading can render unclean when it is a day old. This is some sort of gloss of M. 1:3, showing that M. 1:3 is defective.]

[2. T. 1:4: Belongs to Aqiba + Ishmael.]

[3. M. 1:5-6: Belongs to Aqiba.]

[4. M. 2:3/T. 1:7: A priest blind in one eye may not examine plagues. They do not break upon windows to make an inspection of a house + T. Disputes are settled only by a priest with good eyesight. + T. 1:8A-c, which clarify M. 2:3B. The glosses of M. at T. 1:8D-F do not relate to T. 1:8A-C and do not help in assigning the whole complex. But an Ushan principle seems to be operative.]

[5. M. 3:1A-C, 3:1D-H: All are made unclean by plagues except gentiles. All examine plagues, but priest pronounces the decision. They do not shut up a person for two signs at once. The same priest who examines a sign examines it at later inspections. + T. 1:11-12, containing Judah's gloss. + T. 1:13: we take account of changes which occur during the inspection, but not of those which occur thereafter. + T. 1:15: The same priest must make all inspections, but if he died, another priest does so. Assigned at No. 21.]

[6. T. 1:16: If a priest made an error, the decision is null. Attributed to Hillel.]

[7. M. 3:3-8: Period of inspection, tokens of uncleanness, which apply to bright spot, 3:3; boil and burning, 3:4; scalls, 3:5, scalpbaldness, 3:6; clothing, 3:7; houses, 3:8. No evidence of an attribution. M. 9:1-2 strongly suggest these rules are pre-Yavnean. M. 10:1 does the same.]

[8. M. 4:1-3: Comparison of white hair, spreading, quick flesh. No evidence of an attribution. + T. 2:1, white hair, golden hair. Probably attested to Yavneh at the latest by M. 4:7. The issue of turned/not turned, moreover, is certainly Judah's & Simeon's.]

[9. T. 2:5B: Bright spot cleared after certification, with quick flesh and white hair appearing in spreading, is still clean. No clear evidence of origin. T. 2:5A is Ushan, but not clearly related in principle.]

[10. M. 6:1: Size of a bright spot is a Cilician split bean, square; 36 hairs arranged in a square. The square dimension is unattested, but the split bean is well attested at Yavneh, e.g., M. 4:7.]

[11. M. 8:1: What breaks forth from unclean is clean and vice versa. Part of Yavnean construction. + M. 8:4.]

12. M. 10:3: Black hair which grows up in a scall may be located anywhere, but hair which is left over must be encompassed.

[13. M. 10:5: Inspection of golden hair at various points. Same point as M. 5:2, probably Yavnean.]

[14-15. M. 10:6-7: Scall inside scall, parallel to M. 6:5-6, probably Ushan. But SN V:1 strongly suggest it is Yavnean, Aqiban. T. 4:2 attests M. 10:6 to Usha. + T. 4:3 + SN 8:7-8.]

[16. T. 4:7-8: Processes of breaking forth as applied to scall. But T. 4:7 surely is Ushan, in accord with Simeon.]

[17. M. 11:1: Gentiles' clothing is exempt from plagues. See Nos. 5, 21.]

[18. M. 11:6/T. 5:7, 8, 9: Re patch-test: If one attaches a patch from a garment which has been shut up onto a clean garment, etc. Parallel: M. 13:5/T. 6:12: Leazar b. R. Simeon attests.]

19. M. 11:10: Relationship of standing warp and web re plagues. The principle, T. 5:12, is that so long as further weaving will take place, there is connection. + T. 5:13A.

20. M. 11:11A-E. What is susceptible to corpse-uncleanness is susceptible to plagues. + T. 5:13B.

[21. M. 12:1: All houses are susceptible, except gentiles'. See Nos. 5, 17. The definitions of the susceptible house, T. 6:3. 4, M. 12:2, are entirely unattested. But M. 12:3 which is Yavnean, glosses M. 12:2, so too M. 12:4, which is Ushan. T. 7:1 is in the same stratum as M. 12:2.]

22-23. M. 12:6-7: Rules of priestly inspection, plastering, etc., demolishing.

24. M. 13:4: Quarantined house is unclean inside. One certified unclean is unclean outside too. + T. 7:4A, 6:11.

25. T. 7:14-16: Strict-rule-construction, comparing man, garments, houses.

[26. M. 14:1: How do they purify the leper? Glossed at T. 8:3 by Simeon b. Leazar.]

[27. T. 8:1: Purification-rites. The same priest supervises the process = No. 5.]

28. M. 14:2A-E + 14:3: Shaving, stages of purification.

29. M. 14:4: Shaving. + T. 8:4,5.

30. M. 14:5: Birds in leprosy-rule. + T. 8:7. (Possibly attested to Usha by T. 8:8?]

31. M. 14:7: = Lev. 14:10-22.

32. M. 14:8A-D: Slaughter of offerings.

33-34. T. 8:10-9:1: Rite of slaughter.

[35. M. 14:10A-G/T. 9:2, 3, 4: Sprinkling oil + blood. Attested by Aqiba, Yohanan b. Nuri.]

Our preliminary catalogue of unassigned traditions is in fact much too long. While formal traits, in particular, appearance of named authorities, suggest that approximately 38% of the entire corpus of Mishnah-Tosefta-Sifra was in fact without clearcut evidence as to origination in a particular circle or stratum, consideration of the operative principles expressed in the several unassigned pericopae changes the picture considerably. For various reasons we can find assignments for a great many items which, to begin with, seemed without a particular location in the unfolding of the tradition. Let us now review our unassigned materials. Items in brackets may be subject to assignment to a particular stratum, as specified.

1. SN 9:14A-C: Son or disciple examines plagues.

[2. T. 8:1 = SM I:5F-G: Leper-priest does not declare a leper clean. This is in harmony with M. 2:5 -- if only in a general way.]

[3. M. 3:3F-G, 4F-G, 5F-G, 6F-G, 7F-G, 8F-G, SN 2*:4E-F, 15:6: We credit the seventh day after an inspection to the preceding and following weeks. Probably Yavnean or earlier.]

4. SN 1:6A-E: Leper is pained by his disease.

[5. SN 2:4: A bright spot is affected by white, not golden hair. A white hair is not a token of uncleanness in a scall. Might be Ushan.]

[6. SN 2*:8: The rule about an unchanged spot on a person differs from that about one on garments. This is obvious and Scriptural.]

[7. SN 3:1B-E: Quick flesh does not have to come after the bright spot -- unlike white hair. Probably Ushan, as is SN IV:1-2.]

8. T. 1:3B: Spreading can be a token of uncleanness even on the day of the first inspection.

[9. M. 11:1E-J/M. Kel. 17:13: What comes from the ocean is insusceptible. What is made from human hair (SN 13:5-6) is unsusceptible. But M. Kel. 17:13 is attested by Aqiba -- Yohanan b. Nuri.]

[10. T. 7:1: A house wholly covered by plague is unclean. The comparison of the several sorts of uncleanness of plagues is carried forward. A scall is like a bright spot, an afflicted house is not. This sort of inquiry is attested at both Usha and Yavneh.]

11. SM 4:5, 4:3, 4:1: Details of dismantling procedures and processes.
12. M. 14:2: Disposition of bird.
[13. M. 14:3: Stages of purification: Corresponds to Usha, No. 31.]
14. SN 12:5: High priest.
15. SN 12:1: Man, woman -- differences in tearing clothes.
[16. SN 12:12-13: Corresponds to Usha, No. 23. Yavneh, No. 22.]
17. SM I:10: Purchase of birds.
18. SM 1:3: Mixing blood of birds.
19. SM 1:7: Bird slaughtered.
[20. SM II:1-3: Leprosy compared to corpse-uncleanness, see Usha, No. 23.]
21. SM II:9: Immersion in pool.
22. SM 2:4: Nazir, priest shave for purification.
23. SM 3:2: When priests can eat meat, etc.
[24. SM 3:1: Sin-offering and guilt-offering. See Usha, No. 35.]
25. SM III:8-10: Location of rite.
26. SM III:3-5: Setting up beasts.

Of the 26 items before us, the following would seem to harmonize with established principles: Nos. 2, 3, 5, 6, 7, 10, 13, 16, 20, 24 -- 10 in all. Of the remaining 16 items, the following concern the rites of purification: Nos. 11, 12, 15, 17, 18, 19, 21, 22, 23, 25, and 26 -- 11 in all. To put it differently, only the following are directly pertinent to the fundamental interests of Mishnah-Tosefta Negaim excluding Chapter Fourteen: Nos. 1 (a Yavnean theme), 4, 8 (important and unassignable), 9 (important and unassignable), 14 (trivial) -- that is, five items, only two of them really interesting. Fully 11 of the 16 items (68.7%) for which we can find no hint of an assignment to a given stratum, let alone an attribution to a particular authority, concern themselves with the purification-rite, and of these, a fair proportion is devoted to principles of the cult only tangentially relevant to the purification-rite of the leper in particular (not to mention the person afflicted with plague).

Accordingly, placed into perspective, the problem of the unassigned traditions is hardly formidable and in no way constitutes an obstacle toward the recovery of the main lines of the history of Negaim. We do not have to take account, in our history, of the possibility of a long pre-history of legal development, through exegesis or otherwise, before the stages of the law demarcated by assignment to named authorities. On the contrary, with the exception of a few facts, e.g., about the square shape of the plague-mark, about the three week inspection, and similar matters, the bulk of the law and in particular all of those laws indicative of logical and conceptual dynamism derive from the period after 70. Of still greater importance, pericopae not bearing the names of individual masters do not exhibit conceptual or logical traits (let alone forms or formulary patterns) different from those which are given in the names of particular sages or in pericopae in which named sages occur. Accordingly, it is highly improbable that the data for the history of Negaim are greatly complicated by the consideration of anonymous laws and sayings which derive from the period before 70.

ii. Negaim before 70

As before, we now have to ask about the presuppositions of Yavnean rulings and their relationship to Scriptures. Unlike our procedure in Kelim and Ohalot, we do not review the Scriptural materials to eliminate from our catalogue of principles and presuppositions those items which certainly derive from the written Torah. For if we did, we should have little left. The development and articulation of the laws of Negaim depend wholly upon the laws of "the Written Torah." No primary theme or supposition of Mishnah seems to diverge from what is explicit in Scripture. This is remarkable, because the primary issues of Kelim, the uncleanness of domestic utensils, and of Ohalot, the Tent which is quantitatively and therefore qualitatively different from the tent of Num. 19:11-20, cannot be discovered in Scripture at all. In Negaim there are three relationships between Scripture and Mishnah. First, Mishnah will simply summarize, restating in its own language, Scripture's rule. Second, Mishnah will either add some details to the Scriptural law or it will ask a second-order of questions generated by that law. And, third, in a few items, Mishnah will either supply its own definition, not hinted at by Scripture, of a Scriptural item, e.g., the house which is susceptible to plagues, the size of the bright spot; or it will present a rule clearly based upon the themes and detailed laws of Scripture, yet not closely related to Scripture, as in the case of the role of the priest, the principle of doubts in respect to plagues, the status of colored fabrics, and the house which shades an unclean house. These items, to be sure, are interesting and important. But by themselves they hardly change the pronounced impression that Negaim contains much Scripture and little *halakhah*.

iii. From Mishnah to Scripture

The impression formed from the consideration of the primary and fundamental conceptions of the Yavnean stratum is that there is no perceptible distance between Scripture and Mishnah. The Yavneans seem to take up exactly where Scripture leaves off, just as the Ushans take up where the Yavneans leave off. Indeed, the correspondences between Yavnean developments of Scriptural roles are fairly numerous and close, perhaps even closer, upon inspection, than those between Ushans and Yavneans. Accordingly, all that Mishnah-Tosefta Negaim seems to intend is to clarify or gloss the laws of Leviticus Thirteen and Fourteen.

Nothing could be further from the truth. What is new and significant in Mishnah-Tosefta Negaim is as striking, in its way, as what is new and significant in Mishnah-Tosefta Kelim and Ohalot. In a single word, what is new in Negaim is the recognition of the *nega*^{c} -- as separate and distinct from the *sara*^{c}*at* -- translated as "leprosy." The secret of our tractate is emblazoned in its title. Omitting reference to purification of *sara*^{c}*at*, M. Chapter Fourteen and T. Chapters Eight and Nine, we find reference to *sara*^{c}*at* in M. only in M. 13:11 (= T. 7:11) a leper who entered a house; T. 3:6, a leper who has been quarantined may circumcize himself and is free of the sacrifice; and T. 6:7, leprosy comes only because of arrogance. Accordingly, our tractate exhibits a strange disjuncture from Lev. 13-14, for those chapters treat *nega*^{c} and *sara*^{c}*at* as a single sort of ailment, *nega*^{c} *sara*^{c}*at* meaning spot of leprosy (RSV: *leprous disease*; LXX: *spot of leprosy*) and our tractate speaks only of one, treating the two as separate ailments. Indeed, T. 6:7 could not be clearer on this point, for it distinguishes between the origin of a *nega*^{c} and the origin of *sara*^{c}*at*, and then supplies a further view that the two different diseases have a single cause, arrogance.

What difference does it make that *nega*^{c} and *sara*^{c}*at* are separate and autonomous, if also correlated and parallel, diseases? The main differences between biblical *nega*^{c} *sara*^{c}*at* and Mishnaic *nega*^{c} are these: first, the two indeed are separate diseases; second, the latter is subject to the examination and determination of the expert, who is the sage, not only at the specified times of examination, but at all times. It follows that the *nega*^{c} is, functionally, the quintessentially rabbinic disease. The Mishnaic laws of Negaim in retrospect represent an effort to rabbinize -- that is, redefine so as to subject to rabbinical authority -- the biblical rules of *nega*^{c} *sara*^{c}*at*, distinguishing *nega*^{c} from *sara*^{c}*at* so as to supply to the former a distinctive set of requirements and to make room, as Scripture self-evidently does not and cannot, for an authority who is not a priest.

To answer the questions for which we undertake the present survey, the unattributed sayings in Negaim do not form a distinct category, marked off by intellectual traits or by distinctively generative ideas. They are random. Whatever stands prior in conception to our tractate derives directly from Scripture. The basic concept of the tractate is all that marks it as other than a reprise in Mishnaic language of scriptural rules and ideas. The concept is that a *nega*^{c} disease is different from a *sara*^{c}*at* disease, and that the rabbi is the expert on the former. If that is what the "oral Torah" is supposed to amount to, then it adds up to nothing of antiquity. In fact, what forms the "oral Torah" for Mishnah-tractate Negaim is simply the primacy of the sage, which is a critical conception of the Mishnah as a whole. Not only does Negaim not point backward to the period before 70, it does the exact opposite. It places us in the direction of those third and fourth century thinkers and their documents, the ones who reframe the Mishnah into a powerful statement of a position the Mishnah scarcely knows, namely, the Judaism that places the rabbi at the pinnacle, the study of Torah at the center of human life, and the Mishnah on the mountain at Sinai. Of these conceptions, the Mishnah, as much as Scripture, knows nothing. In the Mishnah's system Israel is governed by high priest and king, animal sacrifice in the Temple in Jerusalem comprises the center of life, and the Mishnah-*as-such* never gains a myth of origin and authority in its own behalf. So much for Negaim, the most scriptural, and also the most rabbinic, of the tractates of Purities.

CHAPTER FIVE
PARAH

i. Unattributed Sayings

In the following catalogue are listed two types of pericopae. First are those containing no evidence, direct or indirect, as to a particular stratum, let alone circle or school, to which they belong. Second are numerous items for which evidence of attribution or assignment is indirect, in the sense that a specific authority is not claimed to stand behind precisely what is said, let alone the entire construction. It is best to group together all pericopae without explicit attribution, in the language X says or equivalent language, and treat them all as unattributed. The absence of attributive language, we quickly see, is hardly an obstacle to the location of pericopae within the established strata.

Attestation of some sort is indicated by use of square brackets. In parentheses are items not relevant to Parah. These two sorts of unattributed sayings play no part in the study of our problem.

[1. M. 1:2G-I: Lambs -- one year old, rams two. One thirteen months old is neither a lamb nor a man. Glosses: Tarfon, Ben ^{C}Azzai, Ishmael.]

[2. M. 1:4: Sin-offering of congregation, etc. -- thirty days old and upwards. Vow- and free-will offerings, etc. -- eighth day + T. 1:7B. Eleazar, T. 1:18, attests by concurring.]

[3. M. 2:2A-B: Chop off black horns. Eyeballs are no blemish. Attested to Usha by Meir, T. 2:1E.]

[4. M. 2:3E-G: Work spoils the cow if it is done for the owner's benefit, but not if it is done for the cow's sake. If a male mounted -- Judah, if the owner brought it up, unfit. Judah accords with M. 2:3G. + T. 2:3 + SZ [= Sifre Zutta] to 19:2, p. 301, ls. 10-23.]

5. T. 2:4A: Yoke spoils cow whether or not used for actual work. + Sif. Num. 123G.

6. T. 2:4B-G: Redeeming red cow before slaughter.

[7. T. 2:5-6: Comparison of cow, Holy Things, heifer. Accords with Meir, M. 1:1. Probably Ushan or post-Ushan.]

8. T. 3:1: Difference between priest who burns the cow and the priest of the Day of Atonement. Relevant to M. 3:1 (Ushan).

[9. T. 3:4: Supplements M. 3:3C, 3:11, both are Ushan.]

[10. M. 3:7F-8A-B: They would render priest unclean, then he immersed and performed the rite as a tevul yom. + T. 3:7B. Sif. Num. 129A/I assigns this view to Aqiba. But it is probably Ushan, and belongs to, among others, Nathan.]

[11. M. 3:8C-D: Types of wood used for pyre, possibly Yavnean, as at M. 3:9J-K, Aqiba. But it is probably Ushan, and belongs to, among others, Nathan.]

[12. M. 3:10: When cow burst open, hyssop, etc. thrown in. Attested to Yavneh at Sif. Num. 124E, Aqiba: Once fire has caught greater part of cow (without its bursting), we throw in hyssop.]

[13. T. 3:12F-J: If cow bursts on its own, or if it is torn open, it is acceptable. But the hyssop, etc. is not thrown in before cow is burning or after it is wholly turned into ashes. Sif. Num. 124I. After fire has caught most of it, so Ishmael. Aqiba: Once it has burst open = M. 3:10A.]

[14. M. 3:11K-N, T. 3:14, Sif. Num. 124N: Division of ash into three parts. The fact that one part is kept for future rites, as at M. 3:1, M. 3:5, both Ushan, suggests this little set also is Ushan. + SZ to 19:9J-N.]

[15. M. 4:1L-M: Proper garments for rite: White garments of ordinary priest. T. 4:6-7: Attributed to Yohanan b. Zakkai, Hillel. Sif. Num. assigns it to Eliezer.]

[16. T. 4:1E-F, Sif. Num. 123L: Sprinkling must be done by hand, not with a utensil. Assigned by SZ to Num. 19:4 to Yose the Galilean -- utensil not hand; vs. Simeon b. Hanina: hand, not utensil.]

17. T. 4:2A-B: Sprinkling must be sequential, M. 4:2C-D: One dipping for each sprinkling. + T. 4:3A-B. + Sif. Num. 123N/C-E, 123/O, SZ to 19:4X-Z.

18. M. 4:4F, Sif. Num. 124R: Sacrilege applies. [But M. 4:4F2 is Ushan = Judah.] G: Rite done by day, by priest. + SZ to 19:9EE-GG.

[19. M. 4:4H-I, SZ to 19:6X: Extraneous work done by those involved in the rite renders slaughter unfit until cow is turned into ashes, and spoils water until ash is put in. + T. 4:11, Sif. Num. 123J; An act of labor renders the slaughtering unfit. Sif. Num. 124A, 124B, 124C/A, 124P, re water. SZ to Num. 19:2, p. 300, Is. 5-13, I-P, SZ to 19:5A-C. See above, No. 4. Judah refines this rule, which is pre-Ushan. No. 30 explicitly assigns the principle to Yavneh at the latest.]

[20. M. 5:1: Special precautions vs. Judah: All believed to preserve the purity of the purification-rite -- attests to Usha the whole sequence on the haver and the [c]am ha'ares and the reliability of the latter in regard to the purification-rite: T. 4:12-14, T. 5:2, 3. + b. Hag. 22a: Yose, Why are all believed...? T. Hag. 3:19: Nehemiah, Why are all believed...? The Ushan attestations thus are several and firm.]

[21. M. 5:5, Sif. Num. 128C: With all utensils do they mix, even insusceptible ones. M. 5:6 depends on this principle, and is Ushan.]

[22. M. 5:7-9: Cases of trough -- must be autonomous utensil. Attested to Yavneh via Usha: T. 5:9, Judah in name of Eliezer, re M. 5:7J-K, T. 5:10A, Yose in presence of Aqiba. + SZ to 19:17J-L.]

[23. M. 6:1A-F: Ash must be intentionally placed in water, not fall accidentally. T. 6:2 links M. 6:1 to M. 6:2 and attests both to Usha. Following Lieberman, we assign SZ to 19:17C-E to this set.]

[24. M. 6:1G-L: An act of extraneous labor spoils the water, but not the ash. The point is the same as M. 4:4, above, No. 19. + T. 6:1, 6:4A. See Nos. 4, 19.]

[25. M. 6:3A-C: A flask with a small mouth is assumed to contain mixture. Ushan attestation: Simeon b. Gamaliel, T. 12:6.]

[26. M. 6:3D-G1, T. 5:10B: Water must not deprive from sponge, which is not a utensil. Principle is Ushan, as at No. 22.]

27. M. 6:4: Water must be introduced into the flask by something insusceptible to uncleanness. If it is introduced by something susceptible, it is unfit. This carries forward the view that the rite is done in conditions of perfect cleanness, but I see no link to any other pericope, whether or not assigned to a stratum. M. Miq. 5:5 assigns this view to Yose.

[28. M. 6:5, T. 6:3A: The point is the same as M. 5:7-9, M. 6:3D-G, that we must draw water with a utensil. T. is clear that what was originally an autonomous utensil and then broke is acceptable, closely parallel in principle to M. 5:7-9. Accordingly, we have an item which probably is from Usha.]

[29. M. 7:1-4, T. 6:4B-8, 7:1-2: This large, stylistically unitary set is attested to Usha by Simeon, T. 6:5A. Its points -- 1. Intention is not taken into account in mixing (7:1); 2. work spoils another's water, not his ashes; 3. proper guardianship of the water is required, essential to preserving the water from uncleanness -- develop principles attested at Yavneh, see below, No. 31.]

[30. M. 7:5, T. 7:3: He who draws water for self and rite draws for self first, then for rite. The principle accords with No. 29.]

[31. M. 7:6-7: He who borrows rope after using it to draw water may return it to the owner if it is on the way to the mixing, but not if he has to go out of his way. This is explicitly assigned to Yavneh. The principle of extraneous labor is well attested here. Yose attests.]

[32. M. 7:8: Distinction between work intrinsic to drawing water and work which spoils the rite. Yavnean principle, as at No. 31.]

[33. M. 8:1: If we have two guards and one is acceptable, the water is fit. This is not attested, but is in logical sequence from M. 7:10, which is Yavnean. I am not inclined to see the item as prior to Eliezer.]

34. M. 8:2: He who mixes ash into water should not wear a sandal, for if the sandal is unclean, it makes the man unclean. If liquid falls on man's skin,

he is clean; if on his garment, it is unclean and makes him unclean. (+ M. 8:3-7, T. 8:1-6). T. 7:8, 9 contains attestations of M. 8:3 to Usha. I take it these attest the law of 8:3 and the apophthegmatic structure to Usha, but the substance of the law of M. 8:2 is not thereby attested. Still, M. 10:1 makes the same point, but the reason is not the same.

[35. M. 8:9-11, T. 9:7-8: Judah's disputes depend upon the general definitions of suitable water given in anonymous sayings and so mark the anonymous rules as Ushan at the latest. Eleazar b. R. Sadoq has an Ushan pericope at T. 9:8G-L.]

[36. M. 9:1G-I: If liquid falls into empty flask, we empty the flask and dry it off. Parallel to 7:5-4-5, M. 5:2, attested by Simeon b. Gamaliel.]

[37. M. 9:3: If cattle or fowl drank from water, it is unfit. They will drool into the water. Certainly Yavnean, because of glosses of Eliezer and Gamaliel. T. 9:6B: Eliezer and Simeon refer to Gamaliel's opinion.]

[38. M. 9:6: Purification-water and ash should not be moved by boat. Attested by Hananiah b. [c]Aqavya, T. 9:9.]

[39. T. 9:4: Issue attested to Yavneh by M. 9:1, 9:7.]

[40. M. 9:8-9: Purification-water which is unfit renders person clean for heave-offering unclean whether it touches his hands or his body. But one clean for the rite is unaffected. Unclean water affects a person clean for rite only if it touches his hands. This is attested to Yavneh by Aqiba's cases, M. 10:4-5, and by Yohanan b. Nuri, T. 10:1.]

[41. M. 11:1, T. 11:1A: Jar left uncovered and found covered -- unfit. Left covered and found uncovered -- unfit. Gloss of Gamaliel, but not Eliezer, is introduced. Since it is assumed that dew spoils water, contrary to Eliezer's view, M. 9:1, the pericope as a whole both omits and pointedly rejects Eliezer's views, so falls into Yavneh. T. 7:5, correlated to M. 11:1, similarly pertains Eliezer's view, M. 7:10, but follows his principle.]

42. M. 11:2A-C: Matters of doubt resolved as clean for heave-offering are also resolved as clean for purification-rite. The redactor at M. 11:2D-E places Eliezer (Eleazar, T. 11:1B), here, presumably because the dispute is supposed to illustrate the principle. I doubt that the dispute can be interpreted with much certainty and so cannot ask the redactor to supply an attestation. But T. 11:2 has Judah refer to T. 11:1B.

[43. M. 11:2D-E, T. 11:1B, 2: Lattice-work is insusceptible in respect to purification-water. Eliezer: Loosely-fastened boards are unclean so far as rite is concerned. T.: Eleazar; Judah attests to Usha.]

[44. M. 11P7A-F: Hyssop suitable for rite. I am unable to find any evidence pointing to a particular stratum or circle. + T. 11:6A-B, Sif. Num. 124H/A-B, Sif. Num. 129A/C-D, 52 to 19:61-K. SZ to 19:6K is attached and attributed to Simeon, thus the whole to Usha.]

r the unclean they shall take some ashes of the burnt sin-offering and nning water shall be added in a vessel; then a clean person shall take hyssop d dip it in the water and sprinkle it upon the tent... (in which someone has ed, etc.)

ow ask, what, to the biblical writer, are the important traits of the rite of the of the cow and the mixing of its ashes into water?

e priestly author stresses, first of all, that the rite takes place outside of the hich is to say, in an unclean place. He repeatedly tells us that anyone involved in is made unclean by his participation in the rite, thus, 19:7, the priest shall wash hes; Num. 19:8, the one who burns the heifer shall wash his clothes; Num. 19:10, who gathers the ashes of the heifer shall wash his clothes and be unclean until . The priestly legislator therefore takes for granted that the rules of purity which rites in the Temple simply do not apply to the rite of burning the cow. Not only participants not in a state of cleanness, but they are in a state of uncleanness, equired to wash their clothes, remaining unclean until the evening, only then back into the camp which is the Temple. Accordingly, the world outside the cannot be clean. Only to the Temple do the cleanness taboos pertain. It follows rite performed outside of the Temple is by definition not subject to the Temple's nd is not going to be clean.

hat is interesting when we turn to our tractate, is its distinctive agendum of issues emes. As we have seen, the predominant concerns of Mishnah-Tosefta Parah thus upon two important matters of no interest whatever to the priestly author of rs 19:1-10, because the priestly author assumes the rite produces uncleanness, is ted outside of the realm of cleanness, and therefore does not involve the keeping of evitical rules of cleanness required for participation in the Temple cult. By st, Mishnah-Tractate Parah is chiefly interested in that very matter. An important f opinion in our tractate demands a degree of cleanness higher than that required Temple cult itself. Further, the whole matter of drawing water, protecting it, and it with the ash, is virtually ignored by the priestly author, while it occupies much tractate and, even more than in quantity, the quality and theoretical sophistication laws on that topic form the apex of our tractate. Accordingly, the biblical writer rite of burning the red cow wishes to tell us that the rite takes place outside the understood in Temple-times as outside the Temple. The rite is conducted in an n place. And it follows that people who are going to participate in the rite, tering the cows, collecting its ashes, and the like, are not clean. The Mishnaic rities stress exactly the opposite conception, that people who will participate in the ust be clean, not unclean, as if they were in the Temple. None of this derives from ture.

[45. M. 11:8A: Hyssop with which one has sprinkled may be used for leper. Attested to Yavneh by T. Neg. 8:2: Tarfon concurs, Eliezer disagrees.]

46. M. 12:2A-H: If there is doubt that the sprinkling is done from the right segment of the hyssop, the sprinkling is unfit.

[47. M. 12:2L-N: Purification-water which was diminished -- one dips even tips of buds. T. 12:4: Judah attests.]

[48. M. 12:2/O-T, M. 12:3, T. 12:9-10, 11: One must sprinkle with proper intention. The intention must be effected. This is not directly attested. But Judah, T. 12:8, accepting the sprinkling of a minor if he has the capacity to form the proper intention, surely concurs. And, interestingly, b. Yoma 14a links Aqiba's view to M. 12:3.]

49. M. 12:4: Unfit sprinkling in public domain does not produce liability, but it does in the private domain.

50. M. 12:6A-E: He who sprinkles with unclean hyssop -- if egg's bulk is in hyssop, water unfit and sprinkling unfit. If less, water fit but sprinkling unfit.

51. M. 12:6F, 12:7, 12:8A-D, T. 12:14, 15: They do not count removes of uncleanness in respect to the purification-rite. I see no attestations for these illustrations. The principle, in general, is the same as M. 10:1, M. 3:1-3, etc., which require the strictest purity for the rite. M. Kel. 25:9, which concurs with T. 12:4E-F = M. 12:8A-C in regard to the purity-rules of the sanctuary, is Ushan, but I do not regard this as a probative attestation. Assigning this set to a particular circle or stratum is part of the larger problem of conflicting theories on the cleanness of the purification-rite.

[52. M. 12:8E-L, 12:9, T. 16:16-17A-C: Connection in respect to sprinkling. Glossed by Yohanan b. Nuri. This is not strong warrant to assign the whole to late Yavneh.]

[53. M. 12:10D-G, T. 12:8: All fit to sprinkle except woman, etc., child without understanding. T.: Judah says minor is fit.]

54. M. 12:11, T. 12:19: Dipping is done by day, sprinkling by day, etc.

Of the 54 items before us, the following seem to exhibit no clear evidence as to a stratum to which they belong: Nos. 5, 6, 8, 17, 18, 27, 34, 42, 46, 49, 50, 51, 12 out of 54 or 22% of the set. No. 5 depends upon the issue of not performing extraneous acts of labor, which is attested to Yavneh at the latest. Nos. 6, 8, and 18 are only tangentially pertinent to our tractate's problems.

The following focus upon the issue of the rules of cleanness pertaining to the rite: No. 27, totally insusceptible instruments are to be used, a matter of dispute between Eliezer and Joshua; No. 34, liquid does not make the person who performs the rite unclean, but it makes his garments unclean, and the garments make him unclean; No. 42, matters of doubt in cleanness pertaining to the purification-rite; No. 49, unfit sprinkling in public domain as against private domain, parallel to No. 42; No. 50, sprinkling with unclean hyssop; No. 51, we do not count removes of uncleanness in respect to the purification-rite, which is parallel in principle to No. 27, in that the highest degree of cleanness is required. While these specific rules, therefore, do not seem susceptible of assignment, the underlying moot issue -- perfect cleanness vs. diminished cleanness -- clearly arises in materials we are able to assign to defined strata.

Another subdivision has to do with the hyssop, Nos. 46, tied in to the issue of doubtful cases and thematically related to No. 49 and 64. The important item which remains is as follows: No. 17, on how the sprinkling of the blood is to be done. On the face of it, this catalogue does not suggest we face formidable obstacles in laying out the main lines of the development of the law. To put it differently, the problem of the unattributed saying is not problem.

ii. Parah before 70

All rules and disputes assigned to Yavnean authorities take for granted the following principles, which are not under dispute at Yavneh and which also are not alleged in Yavnean pericopae to have been invented at Yavneh:

1. The cow must not be used for labor.
2. A. The cow is not offered in the Temple, therefore is not subject to the Temple's rules.
   Or B. The cow is not offered in the Temple, but (since it is called a hat'at), it is subject to the Temple's rules.
3. A. The cow must be perfectly red by nature.
   B. The cow may be perfected by human action.
4. Details of the rite worked out: Kindling fire, throwing in of hyssop, etc., garments of priest, flaying, collecting ashes, collecting blood. The issues -- if any -- seem to emerge from debate on appropriate analogies of the rite: Is it like that of the Day of Atonement? Of the leper? Is it comparable to the Temple at all?
5. The water must be unadulterated by dirt or other unsuitable materials and liquids.
6. All persons and objects involved in the rite must be free of all uncleanness. The cow is brought to the Mount of Olives in such wise that it never is exposed to uncleanness. A degree of purity even higher than applies to the Temple on the Day of Atonement is required.
7. Purification-water which is suitable and sufficient for sprinkling causes uncleanness when moved. Unfit water does not do so to one clean for the rite.
8. An act of labor not connected with the rite spoils the cow, the water, and all other aspects of the conduct of the rite.
9. All objects used for lying and sitting are unclean for the rite.
10. The jar of water must be in a clean place.

Among these data of the Yavnean pericopae, let us now e
which repeat the obvious sense of Scripture and the Scri
taken for granted; and second, those which seem to reflect
not disputes about the application of principles available to
the first category are No. 1; the supposition of No. 3, tha
which is commonsense; No. 7, which is explicitly stated i
contained in Scripture. In the second category are Nos. 2 a
primary principle of No. 2), not to mention No. 10. What ren

> Nos. 6, 8, and 9: The strict rules of cleann
> participate in the rite and to all objects used in that co
> No. 8: An act of labor not connected with the ri
> to mention the cow and other aspects of the conduct of

These two matters, rules of cleanness different from, and higl
to Holy Things, on the one side, and the taboo against doing l
rite of burning the cow, on the other, form the foundation for

iii. From Mishnah to Scripture

Let us first consider once again the way in which the
19:1-10 describes the rite, the things he considers important to

> Tell the people of Israel to bring you a red cow without
> is no blemish, and upon which a yoke has never come. A
> to Eleazar the priest, and she shall be taken outside the
> before him. And Eleazar the priest shall take some o
> finger and sprinkle some of her blood toward the front of
> seven times. And the heifer shall be burned in his sight
> and her blood, with her dung, shall be burned; and tl
> cedarwood and hyssop and scarlet stuff and cast them ir
> burning of the heifer. Then the priest shall wash his clothe
> in water, and afterwards he shall come into the camp, an
> unclean until evening. He who burns the heifer shall wash
> and bathe his body in water and shall be unclean until eveni
> is clean shall gather up the ashes of the heifer and depos
> camp in a clean place; and they shall be kept for the c
> people of Israel for the water for impurity, and for the rem
> who gathers the ashes of the heifer shall wash his clothes a
> evening (Num. 19:1-10a).

How is the ash used? Num. 19:17 states:

Fc
ru
ar
di

Let us
burning
T
camp,
the rit
his clo
and he
evenin
govern
are th
being
allowe
Temp
that a
rules

and th
focus
Numb
condu
the l
contr
body
for t
mixi
of ou
of th
on th
camp
uncl
slaug
auth
rite
Scri

[45. M. 11:8A: Hyssop with which one has sprinkled may be used for leper. Attested to Yavneh by T. Neg. 8:2: Tarfon concurs, Eliezer disagrees.]

46. M. 12:2A-H: If there is doubt that the sprinkling is done from the right segment of the hyssop, the sprinkling is unfit.

[47. M. 12:2L-N: Purification-water which was diminished -- one dips even tips of buds. T. 12:4: Judah attests.]

[48. M. 12:2/O-T, M. 12:3, T. 12:9-10, 11: One must sprinkle with proper intention. The intention must be effected. This is not directly attested. But Judah, T. 12:8, accepting the sprinkling of a minor if he has the capacity to form the proper intention, surely concurs. And, interestingly, b. Yoma 14a links Aqiba's view to M. 12:3.]

49. M. 12:4: Unfit sprinkling in public domain does not produce liability, but it does in the private domain.

50. M. 12:6A-E: He who sprinkles with unclean hyssop -- if egg's bulk is in hyssop, water unfit and sprinkling unfit. If less, water fit but sprinkling unfit.

51. M. 12:6F, 12:7, 12:8A-D, T. 12:14, 15: They do not count removes of uncleanness in respect to the purification-rite. I see no attestations for these illustrations. The principle, in general, is the same as M. 10:1, M. 3:1-3, etc., which require the strictest purity for the rite. M. Kel. 25:9, which concurs with T. 12:4E-F = M. 12:8A-C in regard to the purity-rules of the sanctuary, is Ushan, but I do not regard this as a probative attestation. Assigning this set to a particular circle or stratum is part of the larger problem of conflicting theories on the cleanness of the purification-rite.

[52. M. 12:8E-L, 12:9, T. 16:16-17A-C: Connection in respect to sprinkling. Glossed by Yohanan b. Nuri. This is not strong warrant to assign the whole to late Yavneh.]

[53. M. 12:10D-G, T. 12:8: All fit to sprinkle except woman, etc., child without understanding. T.: Judah says minor is fit.]

54. M. 12:11, T. 12:19: Dipping is done by day, sprinkling by day, etc.

Of the 54 items before us, the following seem to exhibit no clear evidence as to a stratum to which they belong: Nos. 5, 6, 8, 17, 18, 27, 34, 42, 46, 49, 50, 51, 12 out of 54 or 22% of the set. No. 5 depends upon the issue of not performing extraneous acts of labor, which is attested to Yavneh at the latest. Nos. 6, 8, and 18 are only tangentially pertinent to our tractate's problems.

The following focus upon the issue of the rules of cleanness pertaining to the rite: No. 27, totally insusceptible instruments are to be used, a matter of dispute between Eliezer and Joshua; No. 34, liquid does not make the person who performs the rite unclean, but it makes his garments unclean, and the garments make him unclean; No. 42, matters of doubt in cleanness pertaining to the purification-rite; No. 49, unfit sprinkling in public domain as against private domain, parallel to No. 42; No. 50, sprinkling with unclean hyssop; No. 51, we do not count removes of uncleanness in respect to the purification-rite, which is parallel in principle to No. 27, in that the highest degree of cleanness is required. While these specific rules, therefore, do not seem susceptible of assignment, the underlying moot issue -- perfect cleanness vs. diminished cleanness -- clearly arises in materials we are able to assign to defined strata.

Another subdivision has to do with the hyssop, Nos. 46, tied in to the issue of doubtful cases and thematically related to No. 49 and 64. The important item which remains is as follows: No. 17, on how the sprinkling of the blood is to be done. On the face of it, this catalogue does not suggest we face formidable obstacles in laying out the main lines of the development of the law. To put it differently, the problem of the unattributed saying is not problem.

ii. Parah before 70

All rules and disputes assigned to Yavnean authorities take for granted the following principles, which are not under dispute at Yavneh and which also are not alleged in Yavnean pericopae to have been invented at Yavneh:

1. The cow must not be used for labor.
2. A. The cow is not offered in the Temple, therefore is not subject to the Temple's rules.

   Or B. The cow is not offered in the Temple, but (since it is called a hat'at), it is subject to the Temple's rules.
3. A. The cow must be perfectly red by nature.

   B. The cow may be perfected by human action.
4. Details of the rite worked out: Kindling fire, throwing in of hyssop, etc., garments of priest, flaying, collecting ashes, collecting blood. The issues -- if any -- seem to emerge from debate on appropriate analogies of the rite: Is it like that of the Day of Atonement? Of the leper? Is it comparable to the Temple at all?
5. The water must be unadulterated by dirt or other unsuitable materials and liquids.
6. All persons and objects involved in the rite must be free of all uncleanness. The cow is brought to the Mount of Olives in such wise that it never is exposed to uncleanness. A degree of purity even higher than applies to the Temple on the Day of Atonement is required.
7. Purification-water which is suitable and sufficient for sprinkling causes uncleanness when moved. Unfit water does not do so to one clean for the rite.
8. An act of labor not connected with the rite spoils the cow, the water, and all other aspects of the conduct of the rite.
9. All objects used for lying and sitting are unclean for the rite.
10. The jar of water must be in a clean place.

Among these data of the Yavnean pericopae, let us now eliminate two sorts, first, those which repeat the obvious sense of Scripture and the Scriptural origin of which may be taken for granted; and second, those which seem to reflect disputes fresh at Yavneh, and not disputes about the application of principles available to, and shared by, all parties. In the first category are No. 1; the supposition of No. 3, that the cow must be red; No. 5, which is commonsense; No. 7, which is explicitly stated in Scripture; and No. 10, also contained in Scripture. In the second category are Nos. 2 and 4 (which simply repeats the primary principle of No. 2), not to mention No. 10. What remain are the following:

> Nos. 6, 8, and 9: The strict rules of cleanness applied to all who participate in the rite and to all objects used in that connection.
>
> No. 8: An act of labor not connected with the rite spoils the water, not to mention the cow and other aspects of the conduct of the rite.

These two matters, rules of cleanness different from, and higher than, those applying even to Holy Things, on the one side, and the taboo against doing labor not connected with the rite of burning the cow, on the other, form the foundation for the Yavnean stratum.

iii. From Mishnah to Scripture

Let us first consider once again the way in which the priestly author of Numbers 19:1-10 describes the rite, the things he considers important to say about it:

> Tell the people of Israel to bring you a red cow without defect, in which there is no blemish, and upon which a yoke has never come. And you shall give her to Eleazar the priest, and she shall be taken outside the camp and slaughtered before him. And Eleazar the priest shall take some of her blood with his finger and sprinkle some of her blood toward the front of the tent of meeting seven times. And the heifer shall be burned in his sight; her skin, her flesh, and her blood, with her dung, shall be burned; and the priest shall take cedarwood and hyssop and scarlet stuff and cast them into the midst of the burning of the heifer. Then the priest shall wash his clothes and bathe his body in water, and afterwards he shall come into the camp, and the priest shall be unclean until evening. He who burns the heifer shall wash his clothes in water and bathe his body in water and shall be unclean until evening. And a man who is clean shall gather up the ashes of the heifer and deposit them outside the camp in a clean place; and they shall be kept for the congregation of the people of Israel for the water for impurity, and for the removal of sin. And he who gathers the ashes of the heifer shall wash his clothes and be unclean until evening (Num. 19:1-10a).

How is the ash used? Num. 19:17 states:

> For the unclean they shall take some ashes of the burnt sin-offering and running water shall be added in a vessel; then a clean person shall take hyssop and dip it in the water and sprinkle it upon the tent... (in which someone has died, etc.)

Let us now ask, what, to the biblical writer, are the important traits of the rite of the burning of the cow and the mixing of its ashes into water?

The priestly author stresses, first of all, that the rite takes place outside of the camp, which is to say, in an unclean place. He repeatedly tells us that anyone involved in the rite is made unclean by his participation in the rite, thus, 19:7, the priest shall wash his clothes; Num. 19:8, the one who burns the heifer shall wash his clothes; Num. 19:10, and he who gathers the ashes of the heifer shall wash his clothes and be unclean until evening. The priestly legislator therefore takes for granted that the rules of purity which govern rites in the Temple simply do not apply to the rite of burning the cow. Not only are the participants not in a state of cleanness, but they are in a state of uncleanness, being required to wash their clothes, remaining unclean until the evening, only then allowed back into the camp which is the Temple. Accordingly, the world outside the Temple cannot be clean. Only to the Temple do the cleanness taboos pertain. It follows that a rite performed outside of the Temple is by definition not subject to the Temple's rules and is not going to be clean.

What is interesting when we turn to our tractate, is its distinctive agendum of issues and themes. As we have seen, the predominant concerns of Mishnah-Tosefta Parah thus focus upon two important matters of no interest whatever to the priestly author of Numbers 19:1-10, because the priestly author assumes the rite produces uncleanness, is conducted outside of the realm of cleanness, and therefore does not involve the keeping of the Levitical rules of cleanness required for participation in the Temple cult. By contrast, Mishnah-Tractate Parah is chiefly interested in that very matter. An important body of opinion in our tractate demands a degree of cleanness higher than that required for the Temple cult itself. Further, the whole matter of drawing water, protecting it, and mixing it with the ash, is virtually ignored by the priestly author, while it occupies much of our tractate and, even more than in quantity, the quality and theoretical sophistication of the laws on that topic form the apex of our tractate. Accordingly, the biblical writer on the rite of burning the red cow wishes to tell us that the rite takes place outside the camp, understood in Temple-times as outside the Temple. The rite is conducted in an unclean place. And it follows that people who are going to participate in the rite, slaughtering the cows, collecting its ashes, and the like, are not clean. The Mishnaic authorities stress exactly the opposite conception, that people who will participate in the rite must be clean, not unclean, as if they were in the Temple. None of this derives from Scripture.

CHAPTER SIX
TOHOROT

i. Unattributed Sayings

In order to make very clear the preponderance of evidence for the attribution of pericopae lacking attributive formulas, I marked them with an asterisk, the wholly unattributed pericopae, those with attestation of some sort in brackets.

[1. M. 1:4: Attested by Judah at M. Hul. 9:1.]

[2-3. M. 1:7-8: If something is connected to another object and the latter is made unclean, the former is unclean equally. But if we attach something to an unclean object, it shares in the uncleanness of the object to which it is connected only so long as it is connected. Thereafter it is a remove less, by virtue of its former connection only. M. 1:7-8/T. 1:2 are unattributed. But the parallel problems of Kelim are attributed to Ushans, e.g., M. Kel. 28:6 (Part II, pp. 310-312); M. 27:9-10 (Part II, pp. 291-293), M. Kel. 18:6-8 (Part II, pp. 132-138); M. Kel. 19:5-6 (Part II, pp. 157-160), etc. The principle of these scattered examples is the same as that of M. 1:7-8.]

[4. M. 1:9/T. 1:7B: The point is the same as M. 2:6, which is Ushan.]

[5. M. 2:1: attested to Usha by T. 1:3, 4.]

[6. M. 2:2C-D, M. 2:3-7, M. 2:8: Eleazar of M. 2:7 does not help us to assign this group, but Eleazar b. R. Sadoz of M. 2:8C-D, on the one side, and Aqiba, M. Sot. 5:2, do. Aqiba's issue is the same as M. 2:3-6: Does unconsecrated food in the second remove produce uncleanness at the third remove? Accordingly, M. 2:7's Eleazar, and M. 2:3-6's anonymous rule, disagree on an issue live at Yavneh. The secondary issue, M. 2:2C-D and M. 2:8B-D, the status of food prepared as if it fell into a higher remove of uncleanness, is Ushan. + T. 1:5.]

[7. T. 1:6C-F, 1:7A: These pericopae continue T. 1:5, glossing M. 2:3-5. They are probably Ushan at the latest.]

[8. M. 3:1, 2D-H, 3, + M. 10:5: The main point of this set is that when something solid exactly at the volume needed to impart uncleanness begins to melt, the liquid is not contaminated, since the solid is no longer of requisite volume to impart uncleanness to the exuding liquid. T. 11:10-11 has a clear Ushan attestation, Yose.]

[9-12. T. 2:4-7: Three traits in respect to liquids. The main point in this major set has to do with when something is liquid or solid and the affect of intention on both. The main legal principles are attested by Simeon at T. 3:1.]

*13-14. T. 3:2-3: The main point is the same as M. 9:1 re wanted and unwanted liquids' capacity to render something unclean. T. 3:3: Refinements of issues of unclean liquids.

*15. M. 3:4: The point is the same as M. 3:1, etc., above, No. 8. What shrinks to less than the bulk of an egg does not impart uncleanness.

[16. M. 3:5: All unclean things are adjudged in accord with their state when found. M. 9:9, 10:7 reverts to this principle. It contains the scorched rag of M. Kel. 27:11, an Ushan item. + T. 3:4, 5, 6. + M. 4:4E-H, M. 4:1, T. 5:8A, etc. seem to depend on this principle and are Ushan. M. 5:6 cites it explicitly and is Ushan. M. 8:3/T.9:8-9, Ushan, also cite it. M. 10:7 depends on M. 3:5 also.)

[17. M. 3:6: Attested to Usha by Simeon, T. 3:. + M. 3:7, itself attested to Usha at M. 3:8 by Meir. + T. 3:11, 12 [Yose].]

[18. T. 3:8-10: Attested to Usha by Judah.]

[19. M. 4:2-3: If an unclean thing has an abiding place, matter of doubt is deemed unclean. Attested to Usha by Judah, M. 4:1. + M. 4:4A-D, T. 3:14.]

[20. T. 3:14: Whatever is suspended or dragged -- matter of doubt deemed unclean. Whatever is thrown -- matter of doubt deemed clean. Attested to Usha by M. 4:1.]

[21. T. 4:3: The issue is apparently interrogation, attested to Usha at M. 3:6.]

[22. T. 4:4: Accords with M. 3:5.]

[23. T. 4:7: Retroactive contamination. T. depends on M. 4:3, which is Ushan.]

*24. T. 4:9: Retroactive contamination by grave.

*25. T. 4:10: Whatever is discovered in something which is boiling, even though there is no liquid on it, is unclean. What is found in cold broth, even though there is flowing liquid on it, is clean.

[26. M. 4:5A-B: On account of six matters of doubt do they burn heave-offering. Attested by Yose.]

[27. M. 4:6: Attested to Usha by M. 4:5.]

[28. M. 4:7 + 8-13: Attested to Usha at M. 4:8, 10, T. 5:6, 5:7, 5:8A. + T. 11:14.]

*29. T. 5:17: Importance of consulting sages right away.

[30. T. 6:2: Nine creeping things and one frog, etc. -- we deem doubt in public domain to be clean, in private domain, unclean. Since Simeon b. Gamaliel, T. 6:1, holds a contrary view, this too is Ushan.]

[31-38. M. 5:3-4, 5-6: Since M. 5:5-6 depend on exactly the case of M. 5:3-4, sharing a common protasis, we are probably on firm ground in assigning M. 5:3-4 to Usha. + T. 6:3, 4, 5, 6. Furthermore, M. 5:3-4 give one example of the principle of Judah, M. 5:-6.]

[39. T. 6:11: Cites M. 5:7A-D, which belong to an Ushan pericope.]

[40-44. M. 5:9, T. 6:13-16: Attested to Usha by Meir.]

[45-46. T. 7:10-11: Continues theory of M. 6:6/T 7:9, which is Ushan.]

[47. M. 6:7/T. 7:8: Probably Ushan, the primary distinction being attested to Usha by M. 6:8-9.]

[48. T. 8:3: Haver who said to ^{c}am ha'ares, Go sleep in house... Ushan problem, parallel to M. 7:2-4.]

[49-50 M. 7:5/T. 8:7A: He who leaves ^{c}am ha'ares in house to guard it -- when owner sees those that enter and leave, etc. This is the same theme as M. 7:1-4 and is probably Ushan.]

[51-53. M. 7:6/T. 8:5-6: T. 8:5-6: T. 8:6 assigns M. 7:6A-B to Meir.]

*54. M. 7:7D-E: He who leaves utensils from one vintage to the next -- clean.

*55. T. 8:9: He who purchases... and he who gives over....

[56. T. 9:2: Re ^{c}am ha'ares/haver in courtyard. This continues Ushan materials.]

[57-58. M. 8:2D-D: Context is Ushan. + T. 9:4.]

[59. M. 8:3: Attested to Usha by T. 9:8-9: Simeon.]

[60. T. 9:12A: Augments M. 8:3M, Ushan pericope.]

[61. M. 8:5: The issue is the same as M. 7:1E-F: What is ^{c}am ha'ares assumed to do. Rejects Simeon's view, T. 8:1.]

[62. T. 9:15A-D: Context is Ushan problem of M. 8:8A.]

[63. M. 9:2-3A-C: Probably attested to Yavneh by Eliezer's dispute, M. 9:3C-K. In any event M. 9:2-3 interpret and spell out Gamaliel's view, M. 9:1, on susceptibility of olives.]

[64. T. 10:4: Supplements M. 9:3A-C, which spells out Gamaliel's opinion.]

*65-67. T. 10:5, 6, 7: This group is autonomous of M. T. 10:5 concurs with, but does not allude to or depend on, M. 9:2A. T. 10:6-7 are wholly autonomous of M.

[68. M. 9:6: The issue is whether exuded moisture is desired, a principle assigned to the Houses.]

[69. M. 9:8/M. 10:2: Creeping thing found in millstones -- unclean is only place which it touches. We accept testimony of workers as at M. 10:2. Neither M. 9:8 nor M. 10:2 is attested, but M. 10:3, which is Ushan, covers exactly the same ground.]

[70. M. 9:9: Attested to the period after Usha by T. 10:11B, 12A; 11:1.]

[71. T. 11:6-7: He who weighs grapes -- even though liquid flows, etc. Principle is that liquid which is not wanted is insusceptible.]

*72-73. M. 10:6/T. 11:12: If spit of an ^{c}am ha'ares may or may not have fallen into pit....

[74. M. 10:7/T. 11:13: Emptying cistern. Probably Ushan, in line with M. 3:5.]

[75. M. 10:8/T. 11:15-16: Attested to Usha by Yose, M. 10:81, Simeon b. Gamaliel, T. 11:16K.]

Of the 75 items in our catalogue, we find that the following bear no clear evidence of attestation, let alone attribution: Nos. 13-14, 15, 24, 25, 29, 54, 55, 65-67, 72-73 -- 17%. But of that small nunber, we have to eliminate Nos. 13-14, the principle of which is assigned (rightly or wrongly) to the Houses; and 15, which takes for granted that what is less than bulk of an egg does not impart uncleanness -- Ushan at the latest. That leaves no more than ten items -- 13%.

Of the remaining unattested materials, Nos. 24, 25, 29 do not fall within the legal framework of our tractate. The remaining items, moreover, deal with attested themes and principles. That is to say, Nos. 54-5, 65-67, 72-73 -- all that remain -- rely upon familiar distinctions or principles and fit within the thematic structure of their respective chapters, constituting refinements, not autonomous and independent rules. The problem of unattributed pericopae for the present tractate is negligible. The possibility that rules lacking attributions derive from the period before 70 is nil. It is exceedingly difficult to discover in unattributed materials detailed conceptions not entirely familiar in attributed ones. That fact, still more than the negligible number of such items, is decisive evidence that for the present tractate there is no probability whatsoever that unattributed materials go back to some long anonymous period before 70 and preserve "very early" law. This is a young tractate, and the anonymous and unassignable materials appear, in the main, to reveal conceptions, in detail, well attested only in second century pericopae.

ii. Tohorot before 70

The Yavnean materials on doubts and on the ^cam ha'ares are so sparse that it is difficult to determine what, if any, conceptions deriving from the period before 70 form the substratum of laws on those matters. It seems probable that a formula, doubt about plagues/clean, stands behind the exemplifications of doubts in Negaim. (M. Neg. 4:11-5:1); I see no reason that a formula requiring specification and differentiation, such as doubts about uncleannesses/clean/unclean should not have come down from masters before 70. But if that is what did come down, and is what is clarified in the distinction between public and private domain, then it is not a prepossessing tradition. Like the Ushans' effort to figure out what to do with doubts about liquids/clean + / - unclean, the creative work on the matter is that of the exegetes of the inherited formula. And even such an obscure formula as the foregoing does not appear to have been received in connection with the ^cam ha'ares. Self-evidently, the certain heritage of the period before 70 is of a different order: the conception that people who keep clean must avoid contamination by people who do not. But that matter is inherent in the very structure of the law. The articulation of the matter in terms of assessing what the ^cam ha'ares will and will not likely do in one or another circumstance seems to begin, at the earliest, in later Yavnean circles; but most of the work is Ushan.

Self-evidently, with the cleanness of foods and liquids, and the conception of removes of uncleanness, levels of sanctification, Yavneans deal with conceptions of considerable sophistication. The major ideas are not merely generalities, as with the ^{c}am ha'ares, -- he will or will not do so and so, multiplied in dozens of instances -- but in conceptual density. One matter, minor to be sure, which, I take for granted, derives from the period before 70 is the conception that food must be of the bulk of an egg to impart uncleanness. A second, and one generative of the dynamic of Mishnah's laws, is the conception of removes of uncleanness, on the one hand, and the variations among unconsecrated food, heave-offering, and Holy Things, in respect to receiving or imparting uncleanness, on the other. This last aspect -- receiving or imparting uncleanness -- is under debate, therefore in process of development, at Yavneh. It is highly unlikely that any sort of antecedent tradition on the subject was available. This is the meaning of sayings attributed to Yohanan b. Zakkai by Joshua, to Aqiba, to Eleazar, and to Eliezer, in the several contexts. The sayings deal with most elementary questions, e.g., the capacity of unconsecrated food in various removes to impart uncleanness and the like.

Do the later rabbis attribute to authorities before 70 the conception of removes of uncleanness and the related matter of the affects upon unconsecrated food, heave-offering, and Holy Things, of food unclean at the several removes? A review of the materials assembled in The Rabbinic Traditions about the Pharisees before 70 shows that not a single pericope attributed to named authorities before 70 or to the Houses makes significant reference to the issue of removes, whether or not in relationship to the differentiation of unconsecrated food, heave-offering, and Holy Things. Sifra's exegeses in which the concept of removes occurs are assigned to Aqiba, as at M. Sot. 5:2 (T. Sot. 5:13) (Shemini VII:12) and still later authorities (Sav. 9:2). This of course cannot prove that the twin-conceptions were not thought of before 70. But it does make it difficult to demonstrate that the notion was subjected to deep analysis in pre-Yavnean times. The upshot is that the primary conceptions of the Yavnean stratum of law on removes of uncleanness and their relationship to the levels of sanctification of foods and liquids take shape in Yavneh itself.

iii. From Mishnah to Scripture

The tractate at hand bears no direct relationship to Scripture. None of its generative conceptions relates to any verse of Scripture.

CHAPTER SEVEN
MIQVAOT

i. Unattributed Sayings

The absence of attributive language is hardly an obstacle to the location of pericopae within the established strata. In order to make very clear the preponderance of evidence for the attribution of pericopae lacking attributive formulas, I mark the wholly unattributed pericopae with asterisks, those with attestation of some sort in brackets.

*1. M. 1:1A-B, 1:6A-B, 7-8/T. 1:13B (rain drippings), 1:15: Six grades of gathering water: 1. water of rain-drippings which have ceased (and equivalents) vs. 2. water of rain-drippings which have not ceased; 3. pool with forty seahs; 4. spring with sparse water, augmented by drawn water; 5. smitten spring-water; 6. living water. The basic structure is not attested.

+ M. 1:4T: All same are water of ponds, cisterns, ditches, caverns, rain-drippings which have ceased and immersion-pools lacking forty seahs. The view that the forty seahs must be still, not flowing, is attested to Usha by T. 3:4B.

+ M. 5:3: Spring drawn out like centipede -- affect of drawn water added to augment flow (= M. 1:7). + T. 4:9 = T. 1:15.

+ M. 5:4: Ushan items, re salty = smitten spring water, M. 1:8. Definitely Ushan, see Meir, Yose, Judah No. 1.

+ M. 5:6: Dip or dunk in any place in which are forty seahs = M. 1:7.

+ Sifra Shemini IX: 1,3 = M. 1:7-8.

*2. T. 1:3: Pond into which wine, honey or milk has fallen -- they follow the majority. If olive-oil fell, even congealed, pool is unclean...

*3. T. 1:4: Wine of heave-offering which fell on fruit -- rinsed off. Olive oil of heave-offering which fell one wine -- skimmed off.

[4. T. 1:5: Mud and puddles by doors of shops in public domain in rainy season assumed clean. Depends on M. 1:4U-Y, which is Ushan.]

*5. T. 1:14: He who digs at side of ocean, river -- water is like rain-pond. Depends on M. 1:6-7.

[6. M. 2:3: Doubt about drawn waters which sages declared clean -- issue is whether or not we can attribute the case so as to rule in favor of cleanness. + T. 2:1, 2, 3, 4. This is probably Ushan, because its source, M. Toh. 4:7, is certainly Ushan. Yose, T. 2:5D-K, takes M. 2:3 for granted. Meir's set, T. 2:6-12, further attests to Usha.]

[7. M. 4:2: He who leaves tray under waterspout -- if it has rim, unfit. If not, fit. Surely accords with Houses, M. 4:1. + T. 4:1. M. 5:2 strongly suggests this is an Ushan concern.]

[8. M. 4:4: Drawn water and rain-water which mingled in courtyard -- if greater part fit -- fit; unfit -- unfit. This is when they mingle before they reach pool. Attested to Usha by T. 4:3, Eliezer b. Jacob.]

[9. M. 4:5A-L: Trough hewn in rock remains a trough. Utensil attached to rock remains utensil. = M. Par. 5:7, which is attested to Yavneh via Usha, see Part X, p. 121.]

[10. M. 5:1: Spring passed over trough is unfit. Affect of utensil on spring is parallel to T. 3:1, utensil's affect upon rain-water. Probably Ushan. + T. 4:8A, special case. M. 5:2 continues this item and is Ushan.]

[11. M. 5:6: Wave which broke off and which contains forty seahs and fell on men, utensils -- they are clean. + T. 4.5. I do not see any clear attestation for this problem. Not immersing in air, however, is attested to Usha by M. 5:2D.]

[12. T. 4:8C: Water in furrows -- parallel, I think, to M. 6:9, wall between pools which flows over wall, attested in context to Usha.]

[13. M. 6:1A-D: Attested to Usha by Judah's gloss.]

[14. M. 6:2/T. 5:3: Bucket full of utensils which one dunked -- they are clean. If one did not immerse the bucket, water is not mingled unless there is a hole in the bucket. The parallel in principle is M. 10:1/T. 6:20-24, Yavnean.]

*15. M. 6:3/T. 3:7: Three pools, each with twenty seahs, with drawn water at side -- suitably mixed through touching. If drawn water is in middle, not mixed.

[16. M. 6:4: Sponge, bucket with three logs of drawn water which fell into pool -- fit, for they said only, Three logs which fell. Yavnean, as at M. 3:3.]

*17. M. 6:6/T. 5:4A: Earthenware utensil in pool -- if one dunked utensils in it, they are clean of former uncleanness and unclean because of airspace of utensil. + Hands. This is unattested in a formal way, but in fact merely applies the principles that clay utensils are not cleaned through immersion and that hands are made unclean in airspace of unclean oven (M. Yad. 3:3). Nothing important for Miqvaot is contained here.

[18. M. 6:7A-H/T. 5:4B: Spout of waterskin defined. This is attested by M. 6:1, which is cited.]

[19. M. 6:8/T. 5:5: This seems adequately attested to Yavneh by Eleazar b. ᶜAzariah, M. 3:2. + Sifra Shemini IX:2: Principle of cleaning pool.]

[20. M. 7:2: Drawn water spoils pool -- surely Yavnean at latest, b. Shab. 13b.]

[21. M. 7:2-4/T. 5:9, 10, 11: Affect of other liquids, beside water, on pool is attested to Usha by Sifra Shemini IX:4, as well as by the attributions to Yose.]

[22. T. 5:14/M. 7:7: Attested to Usha by Judah, T. 5:14.]

[23. T. 6:4: Bath whose attendants are gentiles, etc. Continues the issue of T. 6:2-3, gentile baths in Land of Israel. Probably Ushan.]

[24. M. 8:5A-C: Menstruating woman who placed coins in mouth and immersed -- clean from former uncleanness but unclean because of spit. Attested to Usha by M. Kel. 8:10.]

[25. M. 9:1-4: The construction is Ushan. Judah, 9:1, does not attest. But Yose, 9:2G, attests clay. + T. 6:9. T. 6:10 includes Jonathan b. Joseph. + T. 6:13B-14A, Yose. + T. 7:1, re mud, soot.]

[26. M. 9:5-7: As above, Ushan glosses and attributions. + T. 6:15, 16.]

[27. T. 6:11: Depends on M. 9:5A, Ushan.]

[28. See above, No. 13. M. 10:1, T. 6:19, 20, 21, 22, 23, 24 all concern interposition in connection with utensils. T. 6:23 has a positive Yavnean attestation for M. 10:11.]

[29. M. 10:2: Attested to Yavneh by T. Kel. B.B. 2:6-7, Eleazar b. [c]Azariah.]

*30. M. 10:3-4: These do not/do require water to enter in.... + T. 7:2, 3A. I do not see any appropriate attestation, other than the general principle of interposition.

[31. M. 10:7-8A-I/T. 7:5-7: The equivalence of other liquids to water in case of contamination of body but not in case of pool is attested by Ishmael at T. 3:10. The argument there alludes to the principle. The exemplifications of M. 10:8 and T. 7:5-7 bear Ushan attestations, but the principle re liquid vs. water in body re immersion is surely prior to the Ushan glosses of the illustrations. T. 7:8-9A depend on M.]

The problem of unassigned materials is remarkably limited. Of 31 items, only the following contain no clear evidence of attestation: Nos. 1, 2, 3, 5, 15, 17, 30 -- seven in all, or 22%. Of these, the following bear no direct relationship to our tractate, and therefore are not likely to prove congruent to principles attested in other pericopae: Nos. 3 and 17, leaving five items, 16% of our present catalogue.

Of these, T. 1:3 deals with an issue well attested to Usha at M. 7:3-5 -- the status of wine, honey, or milk in a pond. Interestingly, what is important to M. 7:3-5 -- whether or not the wine or milk changes the color of the pond -- is of no interest here. T. 1:14 is a secondary development of M. 1:6-7. It cannot come earlier than the opening list. The principle of No. 15 does not fall outside the conceptual framework of the tractate, so it surely is not a "very ancient" pericope preserved without names because of its unanimous support. The same is the case for No. 30, M. 10:3-4. The issue itself is well-attested at Yavneh; the case itself contradicts elements of the Yavnean equivalent.

ii. Miqvaot before 70

The law of Miqvaot originates in the following fundamental conceptions:

1. Rain-water gathered together on the ground, in requisite volume, serves for the process of purification.
2. Rain-water which has been subjected to human agency, e.g., in its gathering, is unfit for the process of purification.
[3. Diverse kinds of water bear diverse traits, but water does unite or intermingle. This is derivative of No. 1.)

To state matters simply, what is the subject of our tractate? Miqva'ot -- gatherings -- in particular of rain-water by other than human agency (of which the prohibition against utensils is a principal illustration). The gathering of rain-water is the miqveh under discussion. This gathering, or collection, of water, achieved without human agency, further bears the potential of effecting purification, just as spring water effects purification. To be sure, human agency is taken into account, as Sifra neatly states matters, in the digging of the cistern. In other words, what naturally must be done by man is done by man; but the rest is done by nature. Purification is the work of nature, a result of natural processes.

The law therefore might well be summarized in the statement, "Work [done by human agency] spoils the [rain] water," a statement entirely familiar from M. Par. 4:4: "Work [extrinsic to the rite of burning the cow] spoils the [spring] water." Indeed, the fundamental and earliest supposition of M. Parah is that an act of labor is not to be done in connection with the water to be used for mixing with the ashes of the cow for purification unless the action has something to do with the drawing of the water and mixing of the ashes therewith. That conception was highly developed by 70, for the issues raised thereafter extended to relatively trivial gestures. The rules of the two tractates begin in a conception common to both and clearly taken for granted, in the case of Miqvaot, before the turn of the first century C.E.: the role of man in the process of purification is limited to actions or gestures secondary to, but necessary for, the working out of natural processes. These are digging the hole to which rain-water would naturally flow; bringing the spring water to the ash of the cow and mixing it therein, so that, the mixture having been accomplished, the water would take on its supernatural properties -- conveying uncleanness when wrongfully or purposelessly used, effecting purification when properly employed. The two tractates spell out traits of water which effects purification, and, in ways pertinent to each, the diverse versions of the rule state exactly the same thing.

The relationship between the two tractates, moreover, is by no means limited to a general congruence in principle. On the contrary, there is a number of points of direct contact. Central to our tractate is the rule that the use of a utensil spoils water for the immersion-pool. Basic to the discussion of utensils in Parah is that water for the purification-rite must be collected in a utensil. What is required for the one therefore is prohibited for the other. M. Par. 5:5 specifies that broken utensils or broken parts of utensils cannot be used for the purification-rite; our tractate knows that these same objects do not spoil water for the immersion-pool. M. 4:5 of course is shared at M. Par. 5:7. Interestingly, T. Par. 5:8 is very clear that water which flows in a water channel is not deemed drawn in a utensil, and our tractate accepts exactly that sort of water for the immersion-pool. In the matter of mingling or mixing water, M. Par. 5:8 tells us that with two troughs, in a single stone, if we mix water and ash in one of them, water in the second is not mixed. On the other hand, if they are perforated from one to the other through a hole the size of the spout of a waterskin, the mixing in one affects the water in the other. If water overflowed on top of them, even a film of water the thickness of a garlic peel, they are deemed mixed together -- a pericope which is wholly in accord with the conceptions of our tractate. M. Par. 5:9 has two troughs placed close to one another. Water in them is not deemed mixed. If, on the other hand, we so arrange them with plaster or gypsum that the water flows from one to another, the water between them is deemed mixed. These considerations again are familiar. In M. Par. 6:4, a distinction is made between collecting water by something which is susceptible to uncleanness, which is unfit for the purification-rite, and collecting water by means of something which is not susceptible to uncleanness, in which case the water is fit for the purification-rite. We now know that that distinction, which seems to bear no clear relationship to any other rule of M. Parah, in fact is based upon Yose's conception, M. 5:5, that one does not guide the flow of water for the immersion-pool by something which is susceptible to uncleanness. It is no accident, therefore, that the reason adduced at b. Zev. 25b by Yohanan in the name of Yose b. Abba should derive from Lev. 11:36, "Nevertheless, a fountain or a cistern wherein is a gathering of water shall be clean -- its existence must be brought about in a state of cleanness." So the consideration -- to those who hold it in the first place -- concerns both M. Parah and M. Miqvaot, and for the same reason: each tells us an aspect of the attainment of purification from uncleanness by means of water of one sort or another, and the principle of Yose applies without distinction to both tractates. Finally, M. Par. 6:5 is concerned that the flow of running or spring-water not be diverted into a cistern, in which the water will be prevented from continuing to bubble along. But M. Parah explains that the cistern is not deemed a utensil. These are points of clearcut and direct contact.

The rules of the two tractates take into consideration a common principle, expressed in diverse ways. For Parah the use of the utensil is crucial, and so it is, in a negative way, for Miqvaot. The focus of our tractate and that of Parah are one and the same: the use of water for purification from uncleanness; the center of interest in each instance is cultic uncleanness. The reason the utensil spoils water for the immersion-pool is that the flow of the water into the pool is interrupted and no longer follows the course of nature. Rain-water must gather on its own, without human help. Spring water, by contrast, must be collected in a utensil for mixing in the ash. Its normal flow must be interrupted, because, in the preparation of the purification-water, human agency is required, specifically, in the preparation of the ash, then in the mixing of the ash in water. Since Scripture has given the human being a role in the preparation of the purifying mixture, that role is extended to the collection of the water. There is no role for human agency in the gathering of the rain-water, by contrast, and this water must do its work wholly by natural processes. In both cases, the utensil is the crux, the way to assure human intervention for the purification-rite and to prevent human intervention in the matter of the immersion-pool. Uncleanness is the result of upsetting the wholeness, the economy, of nature. It derives, for example, from a corpse or a person who is like a corpse or a person who exudes various fluids. It is imparted to that which is susceptible by reason of its wholeness, completeness, normality, or to him or her who is susceptible by reason of his or her being Israelite. It is, then, removed through immersion in water in its natural state, deriving from the springs below or from the heavens above, unaffected by human agency. Just as it is water which inaugurates the susceptibility to uncleanness of dry foodstuffs, thus, so to speak, igniting the system, so it is water which effects the restoration to cleanness of persons or objects which, to begin with, constitute that natural system to which uncleanness and cleanness pertain.

iii. From Mishnah to Scripture

It would be pointless to catalogue all Scriptural references to water, for Miqvaot is uninterested in water as such, but only in the purificatory power of water under certain circumstances and for certain purposes. Accordingly, what is pertinent is the Scriptural conception of water within the process of purification for the cult. Since our tractate repeatedly refers to miqveh (immersion-pool), let us begin by noting the Scriptural references to miqveh or miqveh mayyim, the gathering of water: And the waters that were gathered together he called seas (Gen. 1:10). Sifra alerts us to the importance of Lev. 11:36: Nevertheless a spring or a cistern holding water (BWR MQWH MYM) will be clean. On the surface, the comparison between the spring and any other gathering of water is invited by Lev. 11:36, which modifies BWR with MQWH MYM, a cistern, a gathering of water.

Scripture knows absolutely nothing of the immersion-pool, containing forty seahs of rain-water which has flowed naturally and not been gathered by human agency. It knows nothing of a special pool, subject to its own requirements, in which washing for the purpose of purification must take place. The Priestly Code does not imagine such a thing as an immersion-pool formed by rain-water which has collected and lies still in the ground. It knows only that when one is contaminated by sources of uncleanness, he or she is to wash in the water, the location, character, and volume of which is simply not specified. The reason it is not specified is that in any event the water does not accomplish the purification. It removes the contamination. The setting of the sun completes the purification. All we learn is that, after certain forms of contamination, a person is supposed to wash in water and await sunset. But the water does not purify.

To be sure, appropriate proof-texts to indicate that water does purify are not lacking, particularly in prophetic literature. Ezekiel (36:25) supplies, "I will sprinkle clean water upon you, and you will be clean from all your uncleanness, and from all your idols I will cleanse you." But Zechariah (13:1) knows only the purifying power of fountains and living waters, "On that day there shall be a fountain opened for the house of David and the inhabitants of Jerusalem to cleanse them from sin and uncleanness"; and, along the same lines, he says (14:8), "On that day living waters shall flow out from Jerusalem..." The prophets, however, speak of eschatological cleansings from the uncleanness of idolatry or other sins. The purification besought by the Pharisees was from the uncleanness described in Leviticus, which had to be removed so that the person might be purified and attain fitness for the cult. This sort of purification is in the here-and-now and for cultic purposes; it has nothing whatsoever to do with purification from sin, let alone baptism in an eschatological context.

Purification for cultic purposes is accomplished, so far as the priestly code is concerned, not by water but by blood, spring water, normally mixed with another substance, blood or cow-ash, and by sunset. Washing in water is routinely said to leave a person or object unclean until sunset, so sunset, not plain water, purifies. Washing in water is not developed through definition of the nature of the "gathering of water" which is required or involved. On the contrary, water is in no way subject to specification and delimitation, since it does not, in any event, effect purification. Sunset does. Our tractate, by contrast, simply takes for granted that when an unclean utensil is dipped in the water in the appropriate way, it loses its uncleanness and rises to the level of cleanness. The same is so of a human being who dips into the pool. Proof that immersion in a pool effects purification is the invention of the category of the tevul yom, one who has immersed and awaits sunset for the completion of purification, as specified in various Scriptural verses. He is deemed clean, yet not wholly so. By contrast, Scripture is explicit that he is unclean until sunset. The contrary claim, in the later rabbinic law, is necessitated solely by the primary allegation in behalf of the immersion-pool.

In point of fact, therefore, this tractate wholly lacks Scriptural foundations of any kind. Its most basic supposition -- that immersion is to take place in an immersion-pool, in a gathering or collection of water -- thus, still water, by contrast to flowing water, which Scripture does know -- is wholly outside the imagination of the Priestly legislator. The Priestly Code refers to washing in water, laundering in water, and bringing into water, but never speaks of the character of the water -- drawn or flowing naturally, or of the traits of the water -- still or flowing, or of the volume of the water -- any amount at all, forty seahs, or whatever.

We have traveled far from the questions that have provoked this study. Let us return. First, do the unattributed sayings in the tractate at hand constitute a single distinct group, with traits that set off those sayings from attributed ones? No, the sayings prove random and miscellaneous. Second, do the suppositions of the tractate deriving from the period before 70 appear, in particular (or at all) in unattributed sayings? No, the givens of the tractate stand in no clear relationship to unattributed sayings. What goes back before 70 among the generative conceptions of tractate Miqvaot in no way relates to the contents of sayings lacking in attributive traits. Third, for the tractate at hand do unattributed sayings bear the fundament of "oral Torah" (as defined in the classical literature)? No, those sayings cannot claim to tell us anything that forms a bridge from the conceptions of Scripture to the givens of Mishnah.

CHAPTER EIGHT
NIDDAH

i. Unattributed Sayings

Omitted are materials not relevant to the laws of Niddah, the bulk of Mishnah-tractate Niddah Chapters Five and Six. These find their place in the logical development of other tractates and in Niddah do not present the necessary contextual substratum of logic and law to make possible the estimation of the stratum to which they belong or in which their suppositions and primary concerns suggest they find their place. Accordingly, for those chapters, the work of distinguishing materials bearing neither attributions nor traits of logic shared with attributed pericopae, from those lacking attributions but sharing traits of logic with pericopae firmly located in a specific stratum, here is not possible. Brackets signify unattributed sayings that do find a place among attributed ones.

[1. M. 1:1G: Every woman who has a fixed period -- sufficient for her is her time. This is integral to the tractate's structure, on retroactive contamination. The principle is Hillel's, that retroactive contamination does take place, but the rule is Shammai's, that that is not commonly the case. +M. 1:7A-I: But woman with a fixed period must examine herself, use test-rags.]

[2. M.2:1B-C: Deaf-mute, etc. -- women of sound senses take care of them, so they can eat heave-offering. Probably attested to Usha by Eleazar b. R. Sadoq, T. 2:9, which deals with the parallel problem for males.]

[3. M. 2:1D-E, 2:2-3: The entire structure is attested to Yavneh by Aqiba. The matter of two test-rags may be earlier. +T. 3:5M-P. T. 3:6 supplies a definitive attestation to Usha for M. 2:3D-E, T. 3:7 for M. 2:2C.]

[4. T. 3:8A, M. 2:4A-B, T. 3:8B: Women who do not regularly see a flow of blood are assumed to be clean without inspection. This theory ties in with M. 1:1G. But T. 3:8A relates to M. 2:3F, the sages vis à vis Aqiba. As above, No. 1, the conceptions appear to be Yavnean at the latest.]

[5. M. 2:5 is attested to Usha by T. 3:9-10.]

[6. M. 3:2A-F are attested to Usha by T. 4:2, 3. +Sifra T. 2:7.]

[7. M. 3:3 accords with sages vis à vis Meir, M. 3:2. T.4:10: Abba Saul also attests to Usha.]

[8. M. 3:6/T. 4:16: The problem is the same as M. 3:5, which is Ushan.]

[9. M. 4:1/T. 5:1-2: Samaritan women are menstruants from their cradles. But M. 4:2 continues the rule and is Ushan.]

[10. M. 4:4A-B/T. 5:8: Attested to Yavneh by M. 4:4C-F, T. 5:7, which take for granted and build on its principle.]

[11. M. 5:3A-E: Girl one day old is subject to uncleanness as menstruant, ten days, Zibah; boy one day old, Zibah. This rule is identical in theory to M. 4:1-2, re Samaritans and Sadduceans, attested to Usha by Yose. In any event, T. 5:14 attests M. 5:3A-E to Usha. +Sifra Z IV:1.]

[12. T. 3:5: Re bloodstains and flux. This is the position of Meir, M. 6:13.]

[13. M. 7:5, T. 6:16: Samaritans' testimony accepted concerning laws they keep. The assigned rulings of the pericope are all Ushan, and the principle is well attested to Usha.]

[14. M. 8:1, T. 6:19, 20, 7:1, 3: Eleazar b. R. Yose, T. 7:1, attests to late Usha or to the period thereafter. M. 8:2: Hanina b. Antigonos attests the same principle to the same stratum.]

[15. T. 7:2: The pericope states the principle of M. 8:2A, which is either Ushan or post-Ushan.]

[16. T. 7:9: This carries forward the clearly Ushan inquiry of M. 7:1-2.]

[17. M. 9:3A-F, T. 9:12A, M. 9:4-5: Attested to Usha by Judah, Meir.]

[18. M. 9:6-7, T. 8:8-11: Attested to late Usha or afterward by Simeon b. Eleazar, T. 8:13; Rabbi, T. 6:13B.]

[19. M. 9:8: Refers to and glosses M. 1:1G.]

[20. T. 8:1-3: Surely a unitary construction and therefore attested to Usha by Meir, or post-Usha by Rabbi + Simeon b. Eleazar.]

*21. T. 8:4: Examination of a woman should be conducted in a lenient way. This is connected, but only loosely, to the Ushan principle of attributing blood to a clean origin or in some way to produce a ruling of cleanness.

[22. T. 9:16: Takes for granted Shammaite position, M. 10:4E.]

[23. T. 9:17: Refers to Gamaliel.]

[24. T. 9:18: Attested by Eleazar b. Judah.]

For those who imagine that Mishnah-tractates encompass large numbers of unassigned and unassignable laws, which "may go back," even in their present fixed formulation and wording, to remote antiquity, long before 70, the present catalogue is little less than embarrassing. We see that, with remarkably little speculation, we are able to find an appropriate location, among the known and defined strata, for nearly every item lacking a name. No. 21 is the sole entry for which, in accord with established and tested criteria, we are unable to propose a firm provenance.

ii. Niddah before 70

A strikingly large proportion of the rules is attributed to authorities before 70 and generates an appropriately sizable proportion of the rules assigned to those afterward. Accordingly, Niddah before 70 appears to encompass a fair measure of the tractate's fundamental structure of themes. The question before us is this: At what point in the period before 70 do the fundamental and generative conceptions of our tractate appear? Upon what foundation do they stand? From what source do they derive? The answer is that our Mishnah tractate begins in Scripture itself and contains no conception of fundamental and generative importance which Scripture itself does not reveal or logically require. The distinction between menstrual- and Zibah-days is clearly made in the appropriate passage, Lev. 15:25. The fact that the former is for seven days is explicit in Scripture. The eleven days assigned to the latter are not; it is the sole matter in our tractate which both is taken for granted and is not clearly assigned to an authority after the fathers, Shammai and Hillel. But it is a datum of the tractate, everywhere assumed as such, but nowhere more than part of the background of facts subjected to the creative work of the legislators. It does not contribute any more -- or any less -- to the tractate than the fact that menstrual blood is unclean. I assume that the eleven days assigned to the Zibah-period derive from the period before the fathers, though I cannot demonstrate that that is the case. But I perceive in the sequence of seven menstrual- and eleven Zibah-days no profound conceptions, no formative and generative notions basic to the tractate's intellectual unfolding.

iii. From Mishnah to Scripture

In Niddah we have an excellent occasion to see how a Mishnah-tractate develops laws beginning in Scripture and conceived to apply to all of the people. We shall now see that the progression indeed begins in Scripture, not in a conception alien to or wholly separate from Scripture, and proceeds, upon virtually no intervening layer of exegesis or mediating conceptions, directly from Scripture to sayings attributed to the Houses before 70, thence to Yavneh, and finally to Usha. Accordingly, before us is a dramatic instance of the way in which, from the turn of the first century A.D., Mishnaic law in a distinctive way spun out commonly accepted rules. To provide striking visual evidence of that fact, we shall consider the matter through tables, each beginning in the pertinent Scriptural rule, then proceeding to list all materials of the period before 70, with their Yavnean and Ushan developments, followed by materials new to Yavneh, with their Ushan developments, and, at the end, rules without clear precedent before Ushan times. It should not be thought that all rules stand in the same relationship to Scripture. In order to show, within each stratum, which rules serve to gloss Scripture, the pertinent, dependent materials are given in underlining. Expansion of Scriptural themes and new rules based upon problems generated by these expansions is printed in regular type. New rules, not clearly based upon, or generated by, Scripture then are given at the end in boldface.

A. The Menstrual Period. 1. Menstrual Blood is Unclean

Lev. 15:19: **When a woman has a discharge of blood which is her regular discharge from her body, she shall be in her impurity for seven days.**

Before 70	Yavneh	Usha
1. Colors of blood which are unclean: red shades. Brown, yellow are disputed.		1. Colors of blood which are unclean.
		Yellow blood: is it a blood at all? Blood of uterus is unclean, of wound is clean.
	Bloodstain attributed to wound, clean. Aqiba: Bloodstains are adjudicated in a lenient way.	Bloodstain may be unclean. It is +/- not treated more strictly than blood. Woman may be Zibah by reason of bloodstain. +Various other applications to bloodstain of rules applying to unclean blood. Attributing bloodstain to uterine blood.
2. Status of blood of a gentile woman [=unclean as a Zabah], of a woman with sara^c^at: Unclean or clean.		2. Status of Samaritans, Sadduceans. They are not gentiles, but also not entirely Israelites. Bloodstains of Samaritans.
3. Does the menstrual uncleanness begin only when blood is discovered, or do we suppose it was present prior to discovery? Examination is required, using test-rags, in this connection. A fixed period means contamination begins only when the fixed period begins, and not retroactively. Use of test-rags.	3. Women who do not regularly have a flow impart uncleanness only when they perceive flow. Vs. women who have a regular period do so. Regular examinations, test-rags.	3. Minors are assumed to be clean and are not examined. Fixed period established through three occurrences of same phenomenon followed by flow of blood.
4. Woman who sees blood on eleventh day, immerses in the evening, then has intercourse, etc. This issue belongs to Zabim.]	4. She who sees blood at twilight is in disarray -- may be Zabah, may be menstruant.	4. --
5. Status of women who die during their menstrual period (or: of all women after death) in relationship to vaginal excretions. Is this blood now unclean as menstrual blood or merely as an excretion from a corpse? (If former, in any amount, if latter, quarter-log in liquid volume.)	5. --	5. Status of blood which exudes from a female corpse. Zab, Zabah, menstruant, woman after childbirth, mesora who died impart uncleanness when carried until flesh has decayed. [Thereafter, they impart uncleanness like all other corpses.]

6. Status of hymeneal blood of a girl who has not reached puberty, who has reached puberty but has had no flow, and who has had a flow.	6. --	6. Distinguishing hymeneal from menstrual blood.
7. --	7. --	7. Blood of menstruant and flesh of a corpse impart uncleanness wet or dry. Zab's flux etc. does so only when wet, not when dry.
8. --	8. --	8. Infants are subject to uncleanness of menstruation, Zab.
9. --	9. --	9. Women are unclean when blood is in vagina, but men only when flux or semen is emitted.

B. The Menstrual Period. 2. Things Touched by the Menstruant Are Unclean

Lev. 15:19b: ...she shall be in her impurity for seven days, and whoever touches her shall be unclean until the evening... Lev. 15:24: And if any man lies with her, and her impurity is on him, he shall be unclean seven days...

Before 70	Yavneh	Usha
1. --	1. Woman imparts uncleanness to one who has intercourse with her (=Lev. 15:24).	1. Man and woman are equivalent vis à vis contamination.

C. The Zibah-Period Distinct from the Menstrual Period of Seven Days

Lev. 15:25: If a woman has a discharge of blood for many days, not at the time of her impurity, or if she has a discharge beyond the time of her impurity, all the days of the discharge she shall continue in uncleanness; as in the days of her impurity, she shall be unclean.

Before 70	Yavneh	Usha	Unattributed
1. Blood of woman who has given birth while a Zabah is unclean like that of a Zabah.	1. --	1. --	1. --
2. --	2. --	2. --	2. Blood in menstrual days has no bearing on Zibah.

3. --	3. Zab or Zabah who did not examine selves on intervening days assumed clean on those days, so Eliezer. Aqiba: Unclean.

D. The Woman after Childbirth

Lev. 12:2: **...If a woman conceives and bears a male child, then she shall be unclean seven days; as at the time of her menstruation she shall be unclean.**

Before 70	Yavneh	Usha
1. Blood of a woman in labor not during Zibah-days is unclean as menstrual blood. This simply attributes to the blood before delivery the same status as blood after delivery: It is unclean as menstrual blood.	1. Woman in hard labor during the Zibah-days who gives birth after labor, without respite, is unclean as a menstruant, not as a Zibah. Scripture is made to say: As at the time of menstruation -- not as a Zabah.	1. How long is hard labor?
2. Woman after childbirth contaminates through intercourse (=like menstruant).	2. --	2. --
3. --	3. She who produces an abortion which was not formed -- Joshua: It is a valid birth. Sages: It is not a valid birth. This is a secondary issue. The child invokes the rules of childbirth -- what about the abortion?	3. Status of a shapeless object. Meir applies Joshua's principle. Sages concur with Yavneh's sages. Meir: An abortion whose sex and status are unknown imposes rules of male, female birth and of menstruation. Abortion like sandal or placenta treated as above, Meir. Placenta imposes rules of corpse-uncleanness, so Meir. Stillborn child imparts uncleanness of childbirth to mother. Uncleanness of childbirth -- male or female? -- of tumtom, androgyne, and abortion of unknown sex.
4. --	4. --	4. Blood of Caesarean delivery is +/- not equivalent to blood of normal childbirth. This is clearly a secondary development.

E. The Woman after Childbirth. The Days of Purifying

Lev. 12:4: Then she shall continue for thirty-three days in the blood of her purifying; she shall not touch any hallowed thing nor come into the sanctuary until the days of her purifying are completed.

Lev. 12:5: But if she bears a female child, then she shall be unclean two weeks, as in her menstruation, and she shall continue in the blood of her purifying for sixty-six days.

Before 70	Yavneh	Usha
1. Blood of a woman who has not immersed after childbirth -- importance of immersion after seven/fourteen unclean days. + It imparts uncleanness wet +/- dry.	1. Status of hard labor during the eighty days of purifying. Secondary issue, combining days of purifying with labor.	1. A woman who does not mark the distinction between unclean and clean days is assumed to be unclean, so Judah.
2. Status of woman in clean days after childbirth: tevul yom? Secondary issue, Does she have to immerse after the days of purifying, or is the immersion after the unclean days sufficient?	2. --	3. --
3. Male completed on forty-first, female on eighty-first -- Ishmael explains the different intervals assigned to the two sexes.	3. --	3. --

Of the items before us, A. 7, 8, 9, C. 3, D. 3, 4, do not clearly begin in Scripture or among the Houses. The point of A. 7 is to contrast the Zab's flux with the blood of the menstruant. A. 8 is new and interesting. A. 9 is Simeon's own viewpoint. C. 3 is the secondary sort of problem popular at Yavneh and Usha. The problem of determining, without concrete evidence, the matter of status is something of keen interest to the lawyers after 70, and especially, after 140. D. 3's issue raises a question Scripture leaves open, about the status not only of the stillborn child but also of the unformed abortion. D. 4 likewise is a logical question left open by Scripture.

These exceptional matters leave no significant doubt as to the history of the laws of our tractate. They begin in Scripture and rise in necessarily sequential and logical stages therefrom. Accordingly, the laws of our tractate clearly begin at the point at which someone determined to undertake a careful reading of Scripture on the matter of Niddah and to draw practical consequences from the results of that reading. The earliest assigned rules belong to Shammai and Hillel, and the Houses, coming later, then Yavneans and Ushans still later clearly work out the implications of the rule of Hillel, in particular. Accordingly, whether or not the historical fathers, Shammai and Hillel, said what is attributed to them, the fact is that the laws assigned to them do originate earlier than, and in striking and concrete ways stand behind, the laws attributed to their successors, later in the first century and even after 70.

If we now ask about the status of the Mishnah as Oral Torah, we find an important result at hand. We are able to demonstrate that the most important facts and generative conceptions of Niddah derive solely from exegesis of the written Torah. The Mishnah bears no autonomous and important ideas that we may characterize both as fundamental and generative (hence as "Torah") and also as distinct from Scripture (hence not written but "oral" Torah.) In Niddah, the Mishnah's ideational structure rests squarely and symmetrically upon the written Torah and rises from it in easy stages of exegesis. So far as the myth of the dual Torah insists that the oral Torah stands independent and autonomous of the written one, the myth finds no support whatever in the facts of Mishnah-tractate Niddah.

The importance of the foregoing results for the present inquiry requires further specification. What we have seen is a striking demonstration that, where we can show the link between Scripture and the generative conceptions of a Mishnah-tractate, that link is formed by logic -- that is, by steps in logical theorems -- and that logic is never made articulate in the tractate itself. (In Zabim I am able to show this in still more stunning detail.) Now perhaps people wish to allege that the "oral Torah" contains the results of that logic. So the "oral Torah" contains a secondary development of what is contained in the "written Torah." I find no difficulty affirming that judgment, so long as it is expressed as a mythic form of logical statement, but not as a historical fact.

Yet the mythic statement bears no connection to the literary evidence in our hand. I mean to say that not a single component of the bridge from Scripture to Mishnah takes form, or comes to expression, in an unattributed statement. I do not even grasp why anyone ever should have imagined that what is unattributed is "very early" and (therefore) a component of the "oral Torah." I find that allegation not only without all foundation in the tractate at hand but also lacking all sense, order, and proportion. In fact it is gibberish. For why should there be a literary aspect to the "oral Torah," and why should anyone have imagined that something lacking an attribution was shaped and formulated and transmitted earlier than something bearing an attribution? My best guess is that the source of the confusion lies in the passage of Tosefta Sanhedrin quoted at length in the introduction. Once Yose's statement was taken as fact, everything else followed. But let the facts once more speak for themselves.

1. Unattributed sayings do not bear in common taxonomic traits to demonstrate a categorical distinction between attributed and unattributed sayings.

2. Unattributed sayings in particular do not bear conceptions that form a bridge between Mishnah and Scripture (any more than do attributed ones).

3. Unattributed sayings in the tractate at hand in no way constitute elements of the "oral Torah," so far as what is alleged to characterize such components of the "oral Torah" may be compared with the actual literary and conceptual traits of the sayings we have catalogued.

CHAPTER NINE
MAKHSHIRIN

i. Unattributed Sayings

In the following list we consider all items not clearly assigned to specific authorities, as well as those in which the role of a named master is minor and primarily important in helping us locate the larger pericope in a given stratum. Items presented in brackets are included for the sake of completeness, allowing the specification of reasons for assignments of pericope which do not bear clear attribution to some specific authority of the major part of the pericope.

[1. M.1:1: The rule is unassigned. It is, however, integral to the Houses' (Ushan) dispute of M. 1:2-3 +4, in that it lays out the parameters within which the dispute is conducted. If the dispute belongs to the period before 70, then M. 1:1 states the primary conclusion following upon the "original" reading of Scripture as to intention in regards liquids. But Joshua speaks to that issue, M. 1:3M, so we cannot take for granted that M. 1:1 -- and M. 1:2-4 -- go back before 70.]

*2. M. 1:6H-K: If vegetables are wet down under constraint, even though the man then deliberately put water on them, they are not made susceptible. See below, No. 12.

[3. M. 2:1A, 2:2-11: This is clearly a unitary construction, laden with Ushan attestations, e.g., T. 1:7, and glosses, e.g., M. 2:4, 5, 7, 8, 10.]

[4. M. 2:1B-E: Human sweat is insusceptible to uncleanness = M. 6:4-5, which belong in substance to Yavneh.]

[5. M. 3:4/T. 2:2: Attested to Usha at M. 3:5A-C, T. 2:3.]

[6. M. 3:8: Attested to Usha at T. 2:4.]

[7. M. 4:1: Attested to Usha by Simeon b. Eleazar's gloss. The principle in any case is the same as M. 3:8. + T. 2:5. T. to M. 5:4 has Aqiba cite the pericope verbatim.]

[8. M. 4:2-3: The point is the same as at M. 3:8.]

[9-10. M. 4:6-7: The point is the same on which the Houses agree at M. 4:4D.]

[11. M. 4:8/T. 2:7: (1) A Father of uncleanness alone imparts uncleanness to a clay bowl = M. Kel. 1:1. (2) Water does not clean other liquids = M. Miq. 10:6-8. These principles are not distinctive to our tractate.]

*12. M. 5:1/T. 2:12: M.'s point is the same as M. 1:6.

[13. M. 5:2: Attested to Usha by T.2:13 -- Meir.]

[14. M. 5:5/T. 2:15: M. carries forward the view of Aqiba at M. 5:4.]

[15. M. 5:7/T. 2:16: The principle is the same as that of M. 3:8, etc.]

[16. M. 5:8: The water falls without approval, another illustration of the datum of the tractate.]

[17. M. 6:1/T. 3:2: Attested to Usha by T. 3:1.]

[18. T. 3:6: Surely belongs on the same stratum as T. 3:5, Usha.]

[19-20. T. 3:7-8, 10A: Belongs with the Ushan materials of M. 6:2.]

[21. T. 3:12: The reason fish are susceptible -- re M. 6:3D, Ushan construction.]

[22. M. 6:4-5: Liquids which impart susceptibility -- attested to Yavneh (at the latest) by Aqiba, M. 6:8.]

[23. M. 6:6: The impart susceptibility to uncleanness and uncleanness. Attested to Yavneh by Eliezer and Eliezer b. [c]Azariah.]

The catalogue contains only one item, No. 2 = 12, which bears no evidence of an appropriate point of origination or assignment. That what happens by constraint is null in regard to uncleanness, of course, is an extreme, contrary way of saying that intention is integral in effecting the capacity of liquid to impart uncleanness. But that does not help us to determine whether the items come early or late in the formation of the law. We notice, also, that the diverse exemplifications of the notion that water incidental to one's main purpose does not impart susceptibility to uncleanness do not always bear attributions or attestations. These assignments (Nos. 8, 15, etc.) are not of so firm an order as those which do. Otherwise, the tractate presents remarkably few formal problems in respect to attributions. On the surface, nearly all items are appropriately assigned, with a good measure of confidence, to particular strata.

ii. Makhshirin before 70

In point of fact, the foundations of this tractate were laid after 70. How do we know? First let me summarize the central and generative theme of our tractate.

(1) liquids are capable of imparting susceptibility to uncleanness only if they are useful to men, e.g., drawn with approval, or otherwise subject to human deliberation and intention. The contrary view is that all liquids without distinction impart susceptibility to uncleanness.

(2) liquids capable of imparting susceptibility to uncleanness do so only if they serve a person's purpose, are deliberately applied to produce, or otherwise irrigate something through human deliberation and intention. The contrary view is that however something is wet down, once it is wet, it falls within the rule of Lev. 11:34. 38 and is subject to uncleanness.

Both suppositions belong to Yavnean authorities. If the tractate derived from Eliezer's circle, we should have no discussion of the matter of which liquids impart or do not impart susceptibility to uncleanness. Since he says that the matter of why a beast is slaughtered, or whether the beast is clean or unclean, is irrelevant, he is apt to regard the origin -- usefulness, intentional drawing, and the like -- as irrelevant. If the tractate came to us from Tarfon's circle, it is at least plausible to suppose that the matter of intention in wetting down produce would have been deemed peripheral, if not irrelevant. In any event, if the opposition to Abba Yose-Joshua had had its way, there is no doubt that we should have no tractate of Makhshirin at all. For what law is needed to develop the simple proposition that what is wet, whatever the source of wetness may be, and however the wetness may happen to come upon produce, is susceptible to uncleanness? Accordingly, our tractate's first principle, its distinction between liquids which do and do not impart susceptibility to uncleanness, derives from circles including Aqiba, and its second principle, the distinction between intentional and unintentional wetting down, assuredly comes to us from Aqiba, in a direct line from Abba Yose-Joshua. The tractate as a whole begins its major conceptual development with Aqiba. What forms its center and unifies its diverse pericopae into a single, remarkably coherent document is the thought of Aqiba on the principal role of human intention in activating the supernatural forces of uncleanness.

The upshot of our inquiry is to locate the primary conceptual development of the first five chapters of Makhshirin -- the dominant theme of the interplay of intention and capacity of liquids to impart susceptibility to uncleanness -- among Ushan followers of Aqiba. The Yavnean stratum, however, is so remarkably slight -- a single saying attributed by Joshua to Abba Yose, and one dispute of Tarfon and Aqiba -- as to render rather uncertain the theory that the Ushans inherit and carry forward Yavnean conceptions. On the contrary, what we find in Usha in the main is the repetition of the two contrary conceptions on an essentially secondary matter, attributed to Yavneans, Aqiba, and, alongside, Tarfon. It may be even that that single stray item is of the same pseudepigraphic sort as the pericopae attributed to the Houses of Ushans. That is, it may in fact also be the creation of Ushans. Of this we cannot be sure. The net result is that the conceptual shank of the tractate Makhshirin begins its history, at the earliest, at the turn of the second century, formed of five layers of conception, in sequence:

1. Dry produce is insusceptible, a notion which begins in the plain meaning of Lev. 11:34, 38.

2. Wet produce is susceptible only when intentionally wet down, a view expressed in gross terms by Abba Yose as cited by Joshua.

3. Then follow the refinements of the meaning and effects of intention, beginning in Aqiba's and Tarfon's dispute, in which the secondary matter of what is tangential to one's primary motive is investigated.

4. This yields the contrary views, assuredly belonging to Ushans, that what is essential imparts susceptibility and what is peripheral to one's primary purpose does not; and that both what is essential and what is peripheral impart susceptibility to uncleanness. (A corollary to this matter is the refinement that what is wet down under constraint is not deemed wet down by deliberation.)

5. The Ushan dispute on the interpretation of intention -- is it solely defined by what one actually does or modified also by what one has wanted to do as well as by what one has done? -- belongs to Yose and Judah and his son Yose and is attributed by them to the Houses.

In point of fact, of course, the difference of opinion begins in the gross principle assigned to Aqiba. We do not vastly exaggerate, therefore, in declaring that Makhshirin is a second century tractate, with roots in the later strata of Yavnean thought, and is, in the main, the work of Aqiba and his Ushan successors and continuators. A tractate devoted to the issues predominant in Makhshirin is possible only within the suppositions of Aqiba. Significant development, not merely restatement, of those suppositions, moreover, is conceivable only within the subtle conceptions of Judah, Judah's son, Yose, Simeon, and Yose. Had the problematic of the tractate been subjected to the development of Eliezer, for the one part, of the opposition to Abba Yose, and possibly even of Tarfon, for the other, there would have been no tractate Makhshirin at all.

iii. From Mishnah to Scripture

The foregoing remarks indicate that the present question is irrelevant.

CHAPTER TEN
ZABIM

i. Unattributed Sayings

Tractate Zabim presents a quite different picture from the other tractates in the Division of Purities. The tractate rests upon a deep and thick layer of suppositions expressed in sayings lacking attributions. Here, for once, we find the conditions posited by the (somewhat complicated) theory of the unattributed sayings as "going way back" and bearing elements of the "oral Torah." To begin with let us review the catalogue of unattributed sayings. Those that may find a location alongside attributed ones that say pretty much the same thing are given in square brackets. The real problems are highlighted, as usual.

[1-3. M. 1:3-5: This set is certainly Ushan, attested by Yose, M. 1:5H, Simeon, T. 1:10, Yose, T. 1:12.]

[4. M. 1:6: Attested to Usha by Yose, T. 1:13.]

*5-8. M. 2:1, T. 2:1-3: This set, on who is susceptible to become a Zab and on the status of tumtom and androgyne, is wholly unattributed.

[9. M. 2:2A-E: In seven ways they examine the Zab. Attested to Yavneh by Aqiba, etc. + T. 2:5.]

*10. T. 2:4: Difference between flux and semen.

[11. T. 2:7: Cites M. 2:3C, part of an Ushan construction.]

[12. T. 2:8-9: Not relevant to Zabim.]

*13. M. 2:4: Zab imparts uncleanness to bed in five ways, bed imparts uncleanness to man in seven.

[14-18. T. 3:1-5/M. 4:6B-J: This major construction is certainly post-Ushan, since it depends upon (inter alia) M. Nid. 5:1, Simeon vs. sages.]

[19. M. 4:1E, 4:2-3/T. 4:5-7: This set bears many Ushan attestations for the distinction between knocking or vibration and shifting or moving by a Zab.]

[20. M. 4:4: Simeon attests the principle of M. 4:4A-G. T. 4:4B leaves no doubt of the matter.]

[21. M. 4:6A/T. 4:9: This matter carries forward M. 4:5, which is Ushan.]

[22. M. 5:1A-D, 2, 3, 6-9 + 10/T. 5:2B/A-G, 5:3. 4. 5A: So far as these items stress the difference between touching a source of uncleanness and letting go of the source, they apply Joshua's principle, M. 5:1E-M.]

[23. M. 5:2-3/T. 5:1A, 5:2B, H-K: So far as these items deal with different modes of transferring uncleanness, they build upon scriptural references. Eliezer attests.]

[24. T. 5:7-8, 9-12: Not relevant to Zabim.]

There are only two major problems, Nos. 5-8 and No. 13. The latter lays the foundations for the shank of the tractate, Chapters Three-Four and Five. Clearly, the Scriptural references to diverse ways in which objects become unclean are taken very seriously and generate much of the law of No. 13. We do not known when the exegetical work produced principles on the modes of transfer of uncleanness, or how these principles unfolded. I am inclined to think the entire matter belongs to the period before 70. The former set, Nos. 5-8, is not attributed. The secondary question on those of unclear sexual characteristics or of dual sexual characteristics in general interests Ushans, but that is not decisive. No. 10 is fundamental to the tractate, and I cannot suggest the point at which that definition was supplied. We return to this problem in part iii.

ii. Zabim before 70

The basic issue in respect to the rules governing a man's being declared a Zab results from the conflict of two available analogies:

(1) The Zab is governed by the rules applying to the Zabah.

(2) The Zab is made such by the flow of a kind of semen, and, therefore, is subject to the rules applying to one made unclean by semen (Lev. 15:16-18). The conflict between the two analogies is inaugurated at the stratum of the Houses, and that debate is carried forward. The unfolding of the law is through concrete and discrete pericope. These interrelate in tight pattern.

But the real issue awaits.

iii. From Mishnah to Scripture

Zabim presents an unusual problem, because the most important conceptions of the tractate appear in units of thought lacking attributions. I shall now attempt to replicate those processes of thought that produced from Scripture -- in a sequence of thought-stages I believe I understand -- the conclusions in the unassigned pericopes. My method is one of analogical-contrastive exegesis. What I shall show is that, in the mind of the exegetes at hand, something is (1) either like something else and so follows the rule of that to which (2) it is analogous, or it is different from something else and so follows the rule of that to which it contrasts, hence analogical-contrastive exegesis. If we follow this mode of reasoning for three or four steps, we move from Scripture to the last detail of the law in unattributed sayings in Zabim. Here too we see that the facts taken for granted in unassigned sayings derive from scriptural exegesis and not from an independent and autonomous source, an "oral Torah."

Once a man is in the status of the Zab, he imparts uncleanness (1) through diverse means of the transfer of uncleanness (2) to various objects: to man, to clay utensils and utensils which are cleaned in an immersion pool and, by contrast to clay utensils, which are cleaned from cultic uncleanness not solely by breaking; to utensils used for sitting and lying; and utensils not used for sitting and lying (= maddaf), inclusive of food, and drink. Further, various body-fluids are deemed equivalent to flux in their capacity to impart uncleanness, and others are not. Finally, the transfer of uncleanness is deemed to take place in two distinct aspects: (1) while a person or object actually is subject to the mode of transfer of uncleanness; (2) after a person or object has ceased to be subject to the mode of transfer of uncleanness. Zabim presents a rich discussion of all of these matters.

A sizable and important group of pericopae stand wholly without clearcut attestations, not to mention attributions. This group futhermore makes distinctions and takes for granted concepts which, I think, derive from a reading of Scripture. Accordingly, as in the case of Niddah, with Zabim it is simply impossible to undertake the description of stages by which the law unfolded without paying close attention to Scripture.

In order to distinguish among the layers of meaning, I lay matters out in a way meant to be visually striking. At the outset, I cite the verse and opposite it restate what it says in simple language. This is given in underlining. The secondary meaning of each verse, given in regular type, is attained simply by generalizing upon the plain and unadorned statement in, and restatement of, the Scriptural verse itself. There is then the tertiary meaning, distinguished from the secondary generalization of Scripture by boldface. This tertiary meaning is the point at which I introduce conceptions drawn from our tractate. I believe that, in the main, principles at a second level of exegesis from Scripture, that is, tertiary meanings, represent little more than a further generalization of what Scripture says, on the one hand, and the (now surely eisegetical) introduction of a few simple and obvious distinctions necessitated or invited by that generalization, on the other. In some instances there is yet a fourth level of meaning, and this invariably is drawn by me from Mishnah-Tosefta.

The exercise is meant to demonstrate that each and every proposition of Mishnah-Tosefta derives either directly or indirectly, through processes of close reasoning, generalization, and secondary logical exegesis, from Scripture itself. At each point at which our abstract exercise produces a principle found in Mishnah, the appropriate pericope is of course designated. The relationship of Mishnah's unattributed pericopae to Scripture is then spelled out in detail in the following section. The net result is hypothetically to demonstrate in close detail that this aspect of the law of Zabim is little more than a logical expansion of Scripture, and that each such expansion stands in close logical relationship to the foregoing, so that the result, at the end, is a very tight sequence of logical-exegetical steps.

My interest is not in the technology of exegesis, but rather in the hypothetical logic by which a rule produces a principle, and by which the principle generates further developments, only at the end inviting formal-exegetical linkage to Scripture. That is, I offer a hypothetical exegesis of what I conceive to have been the intellectual processes by which the results of our tractate have been achieved. Whether or not my account of these processes is deemed valid depends upon the cogency and persuasiveness of my hypothesis of how people thought, and, in particular, of the successive and demarcated stages by which the processes of logic unfolded. To repeat: the principle at hand is that things are like one another, and therefore follow a rule in common, or are unlike one another, and therefore follow diametrically opposed rules, hence analogical-contrastive exegesis. By that mode of exegesis I claim to account for the entire unfolding of the tractate's law.

Scriptural Verse	Clear Implication (Plain meaning)
Lev. 15:4: Every bed on which he who has the discharge lies shall be unclean. And everything on which he sits shall be unclean.	The Zab imparts uncleanness by lying on a bed or by sitting on a chair.

Secondary Meaning

1. The Zab imparts uncleanness to objects which can be used for lying or sitting.
2. The Zab imparts uncleanness to objects used for lying or sitting by exerting the pressure of his weight on said objects.

Tertiary Meaning

A. The uncleanness of the Zab is transmitted by pressure.

B. Pressure is exerted through lying and sitting.

C. Other modes of exerting pressure, standing, leaning, being suspended, by analogy to lying and sitting, likewise transfer the uncleanness of the Zab to another object.

D. Pressure exerted by a clean person upon an object made unclean by a Zab will in like manner transfer the uncleanness from the object or the Zab to the clean person.

Mishnah

C: M. 2:4 (3:1-3, 4:1-7).

D. M. 3:1-3, 4:1, 5, 5:1-5.

Scriptural Verse	Clear Implication (Plain meaning)
Lev. 15:5: And any one who touches his bed shall wash his clothes and bathe himself in water and be unclean until the evening.	Touching the Zab makes a person unclean. His clothes are unclean.

Secondary Meaning

3. The Zab's uncleanness is transferred by contact,
   a. either a clean person's touching the Zab
   b. or the Zab's touching a clean person.
4. One who is made unclean by the Zab imparts uncleanness to his clothing.

Tertiary Meaning

E. One made unclean by the Zab makes utensils unclean.

F. Said utensils are cleaned by immersion.

G. Since Scripture specifies that touching the bed or the Zab (Lev. 15:7) effects the transfer of uncleanness, and since Scripture specifies that sitting or lying also effects the transfer of uncleanness, it follows that these are distinct modes of the transfer of uncleanness, and therefore (1) touching without exerting pressure or (2) exerting pressure without touching imparts uncleanness.

Mishnah

E: M. 2:4

G. M. 5:1-9

Scriptural Verse	Clear Implication (Plain meaning)
Lev. 15:6: And whoever sits on anything on which he who has the discharge has sat shall wash his clothes and bathe himself in water and be unclean until the evening.	Sitting on the bed or chair made unclean by the Zab makes a person unclean. His clothes are unclean.

Secondary Meaning

5. The object used for sitting or lying to which the Zab has imparted uncleanness is unclean in exactly the same status of uncleanness as the Zab himself.

Tertiary Meaning

H. Since said object is unclean exactly as the Zab is unclean, it therefore transfers uncleanness as does the Zab, that is, if one exerts pressure on it (the plain meaning) or if one touches it, or if it touches the clean person or exerts pressure on the clean person, uncleanness is transmitted.

I. One made unclean by the unclean bed of the Zab makes utensils unclean. Said utensils are cleaned by immersion.

Mishnah

5: M. 2:4C-D.

H: M. 2:4C-D (3:1-3, 4:1-7).

I: M. 2:4C-D.

Scriptural Verse	Clear Implication (Plain meaning)
Lev. 15:7: And whoever touches the body of him who has the discharge shall wash his clothes and bathe himself in water and be unclean until the evening.	Touching the person of the Zab imparts uncleanness. The clothes are unclean.

Secondary Meaning

6. There is no difference between touching the bed of the Zab (Lev. 15:5) and touching the person of the Zab (Lev. 15:7). The consequences are the same in all regards.

Mishnah

6. M. 5:1

Scriptural Verse	Clear Implication (Plain meaning)
Lev. 15:8: And if he who has the discharge spits on one who is clean, then he shall wash his clothes and bathe himself in water and be unclean until the evening.	The spit of the Zab is unclean exactly as is the Zab or his bed. The clothing of the person spat upon by the Zab is made unclean.

Secondary Meaning

7. Fluids which exude from the Zab are unclean exactly as is his body or the bed he sits upon, etc.

Tertiary Meaning

J. The ways in which the Zab and the bed made unclean by the Zab transfer uncleanness apply also the body fluids, so far as these modes of transfer are relevant: 1. touching, 2. carrying (below, Lev. 15:10b).

Mishnah

7: M. 5:6, 5:7.

Scriptural Verse	Clear Implication (Plain meaning)
Lev. 15:9: And any saddle on which he who has the discharge rides shall be unclean.	The saddle ridden upon by the Zab is unclean.

Secondary Meaning

8. Since the saddle is dealt with apart from the bed and chair, it is subject to a distinctive set of rules.

Mishnah

8: M. 5:8.

Scriptural Verse	Clear Implication (Plain meaning)
Lev. 15:10a: And whoever touches anything that was under him shall be unclean until the evening.	An object located underneath a Zab is unclean.

Secondary Meaning

9. I take it that the simple meaning is derived by treating Lev. 15:10a as a continuation of Lev. 15:9, which is to say, "A saddle on which a Zab has ridden is unclean, and whoever touches anything on which a Zab rides (or: has ridden) is unclean." But if we read the verse disjunctively, then it bears a different meaning. Mere location of an object beneath a Zab -- even if he is not touching it, and even if he is not riding on it -- imparts uncleanness to the object. Accordingly, we take account of the spatial relationships of objects to a Zab.

10. And this yields the clearly required notion (L) that an object used for sitting, lying, or riding which is located beneath a Zab is unclean, even though the Zab has not sat, lain, or ridden on said object.

Tertiary Meaning

K. Touching or carrying the saddle produces uncleanness, as specified.

L. Touching an object located underneath a Zab, even though said object is not touched by the Zab and even though said object is not directly sat, lain, or ridden upon by the Zab but merely bears the weight of his body, imparts uncleanness so that the formerly clean person is made unclean and furthermore makes his clothing unclean, and, by extension, imparts uncleanness to utensils in general.

Fourth Level of Meaning

i. An object used for sitting and lying which is located underneath the Zab is subject to the uncleanness imparted by the Zab to objects upon which he has sat or lain, etc. It follows that the same sort of object located above the Zab is not subject to the uncleanness imparted by the Zab to objects used for sitting and lying.

ii. An object not used for sitting and lying located beneath the Zab (but not touched by him or subjected to the pressure of his body-weight) is not unclean.

iii. And, it follows in the rule of opposites, an object not used for sitting and lying which is located above the Zab will be unclean, in some way or degree not specified.

Mishnah

9-10: M. 5:1-3.
K. M. 5:8.
L: M. 5:1-3.
i: M. 5:1-2.
ii: M. 5:1.
iii: M. 5:1-2.

Scriptural Verse	Clear Implication (Plain meaning)
Lev. 15:10b: And whoever carries such a thing shall wash his clothes and bathe himself in water and be unclean until the evening.	Carrying an object used for riding, sitting, or lying, and made unclean by the Zab makes the clean person who carries said object unclean. He makes his clothing unclean.

Secondary Meaning

11. The uncleanness of the Zab is conveyed through carriage. Specifically, if one carries an object, such as a bed or chair, made unclean by the Zab, one is made unclean as if he touched the Zab or as if he was subjected to the weight or pressure of the Zab or of an object made unclean by the Zab. This seems to me to follow naturally from the concept of pressure, since it is not possible to carry something without bearing its weight.

Tertiary Meaning

M. A person or an object which a Zab carries is made unclean. That is, just as there is no difference between touching the Zab or being touched by him, placing pressure upon the Zab or having the Zab's pressure applied to a clean person, so there is no difference between carrying the Zab and being carried by him.

N. The person made unclean in this way imparts uncleanness to his clothing, therefore to utensils.

Fourth Level of Meaning

iv. The person made unclean in these several ways makes his clothing unclean. Clearly, that is the case when the uncleanness of the Zab is transmitted to the person. It will follow, therefore, that when the Zab touches or exerts pressure on a clean person, the person is made unclean, and the clothing on the person is made unclean. Accordingly, it is when the clean person is subject to the uncleanness of the Zab, etc., that his clothing is made unclean: "he renders utensils unclean." When the person is no longer subject to the uncleanness of the Zab, he (of course) remains unclean. But he no longer will make his clothing unclean.

Mishnah

As above, Lev. 15:10a.
iv: M. 5:1, Joshua.

Scriptural Verse	Clear Implication (Plain meaning)
Lev. 15:11 Any one whom he that has the discharge touches without having rinsed his hands shall wash his clothes and bathe himself in water and be unclean until the evening.	The unclean person imparts uncleanness through touching. The person made unclean thereby transmits uncleanness to clothing.

Secondary Meaning

I see nothing in this verse which is both relevant to Zabim and new.

Lev. 15:12 And the earthen vessel which he who has the discharge touches shall be broken. And every vessel of wood shall be rinse in water.	Earthen, or clay, utensils cannot be cleaned by rinsing, but only by breaking. Wooden utensils can be cleaned by immersion.

Secondary Meaning

12. Wooden vessels are subject to a different rule from earthen ones. That rule, moreover, will be the same as affects any other utensil which is cleaned through immersion.

Transferring the Zab's Uncleanness: Unassigned Pericopae

Unassigned pericopae, in Zabim, as in other tractates, are those units of thought which contain no trace of attribution and bear no direct attestations. These pericopae lack also the indirect, and therefore probative, attestation which follows when the fundamental presupposition of an attributed or well-attested pericope clearly depends upon the datum of an unattributed and unattested one. The unassigned entries clearly relate to, and I think are generated by, the primary allegation of Scripture or its logical developments, as specified.

1. M. 2:4: The Zab imparts uncleanness to the bed in five ways so that the bed imparts uncleanness to man and garments: standing, and sitting, lying, suspended, and leaning. The bed imparts uncleanness to man in seven ways so that he makes clothing unclean: standing, sitting, lying, suspended, leaning, contact, and carrying. (Compare, M. Kel. 1:3.)

1. The rule is specific, that the Zab imparts uncleanness to the bed in the specified five ways. The second component is distinct. How does the bed transmit uncleanness to the clean man? Omitted from consideration: How does the Zab impart uncleanness to the clean man? In point of fact, the Zab transmits the uncleanness through touching and through being carried (= exerting pressure).

Sifra Mesora^{c} Zabim 3:1-3: Pressure exerted by Zab, even if he sits on top of a heavy stone, imparts uncleanness.

Sifra Mesora^{c} Zabim 2:7: If Zab lay down on chair, sat on bed, stands or is suspended, they are unclean = M. 2:4.

2. Sifra Mesora^{c} Zabim 11: 1-2: Man who touches bed imparts uncleanness to clothing, but bed which touches bed does not impart uncleanness to clothing. Bed imparts uncleanness when under the Zab to impart uncleanness to man and clothing, but man under the Zab does not impart uncleanness to man and clothing.

2. The Zab imparts uncleanness when he touches a bed. The bed touching a bed does not impart uncleanness to clothing. The bed under the Zab imparts uncleanness as a bed, man does not.

Perhaps the several contrasts are based solely upon those established in Scripture, specifically, objects used for lying and sitting located underneath the Zab impart uncleanness to clothing, Lev. 15:10a. Man is not used for sitting and lying, therefore when located under the Zab, he does not. Along these same lines, Scripture is clear, Lev. 15:5, that man who touches the bed washes his clothes -- therefore imparts uncleanness to clothing (= utensils). Scripture is silent on the effect, upon clothing, of a bed which touches a bed made unclean by a Zab. It will have followed that what is stated explicitly at Lev. 15:5 then deliberately means to exclude what is omitted, which is the status of the bed which touches the bed. This is, of course, rather acute, since Scripture speaks of common occurrences, and it is difficult for a bed to reach out and touch another bed; Scripture's use of "touching" naturally is in the context of animate creatures.

3. M. 5:2: Whatever is carried above the Zab is unclean. Whatever the Zab is carried upon, but which is not touched by him, is clean, except for something used for sitting and lying (Lev. 15:10a) and except for man who carries the Zab (Lev. 15:10b).
+ T. 5:1.
Sifra Mesora[c] Zabim III:3-7: Food, drink, utensils not used for sitting and lying which are above the Zab are made unclean on that account, proved by Simeon.

3. The important point here is the distinction between what is carried above the Zab and is carried below him, without touching him. In the former case, there is uncleanness, and this applies, specifically, to food, drink and objects not used for lying and sitting (maddaf). If these are carried below the Zab, they are clean. Only man and bed and chair below the Zab are made unclean because of their serving to carry his weight even without directly touching him.
The illustration, M. 5:2L-M. further indicates that what is unclean above the Zab -- food, drink, maddaf (an object not used for lying and sitting) -- is unclean in the first remove.

The principle is dual: (1) What is carried underneath the Zab is unclean, except for an object used for lying and sitting. (2) What is carried above the Zab is unclean. The relationship to Scripture is not self-evident. On the one side, we may readily account for the first principle. That an object used for lying and sitting which was under the Zab is unclean is specified at Lev. 15:10a. But the rule excludes objects not used for lying and sitting. Perhaps the distinction begins at Lev. 15:9. The saddle on which the Zab rides is unclean. Lev. 15:10a, continuing this point, then specifies that whoever touches anything that was under him -- thus, that has served him for sitting -- is unclean. And, by exclusion therefrom, whoever touches something which has been located under the Zab but which the Zab has not used for sitting is not unclean. Accordingly, the object itself, if not used for sitting, does not become unclean if the Zab is located above it.

But whence the notion of maddaf? That is, how do we know that an object not used for lying and sitting and located above the Zab is unclean? At first glance, it appears that we come to the fourth level of meaning imputed to Lev. 15:10a (i, iii). (1) What is unclean beneath the Zab is not unclean above him. (2) Then: What is not unclean beneath the Zab is unclean above him. Objects not used for sitting and lying, food and drink (2) are unclean above, because they (1) are clean below, the Zab. Thus: Objects used for sitting and lying are clean above, because they are unclean below, the Zab.

But the problem of maddaf is not so readily settled. We have to ascertain the meaning associated with the word in the earliest assigned pericopae. With the help of Kasovsky (Chayim Yehoshua Kasovsky, Thesaurus Mishnae [Jerusalem, 1958], IV, p. 353a), let us rapidly review the several meanings assigned to the word maddaf. The word is familiar as the name of an object, which we have translated bird trap at M. Kel. 23:5 (Part II, p. 220); as the smoker of the bees (M. Kel. 16:7, Part II, p. 78), required by context in both cases. Our tractate, by contrast, knows that word to mean "an object, not used for lying or sitting, located above the Zab," and we need not review the passages in which the word appears in that meaning (M. Zab. 4:6, 5:2). The third meaning is "a status as to uncleanness," a definition to be made more precise when we return to M. Par. 10:1-2, and M. Toh. 8:2. The former (Part X, pp. 164-171) requires the meaning, "A status as to uncleanness related to midras but of lower degree of uncleanness than midras." Thus M. Par. 10:1 states: "Whatever can become unclean with midras-uncleanness is regarded as actually unclean with maddaf-uncleanness so far as the purification-rite is concerned." (There is a further dispute, M. Par. 10:1, assigned to Yavneans, on what can be made unclean with corpse-uncleanness and whether that sort of object likewise is clean with maddaf-uncleanness.)

Accordingly, in the context of M. Par. 10:1-2, maddaf can only mean, "a status of uncleanness," which, we know, is uncleanness in the first remove, effecting uncleanness for food and liquid. This same meaning is absolutely required at M. Toh. 8:2 (Part XI, p. 186): If someone deposits with an ^{c}am ha'ares a box full of clothing, Yose says, "When it is tightly packed, it is unclean with midras-uncleanness, and if it is not tightly packed, it is unclean with maddaf-uncleanness." Accordingly, once more, midras-uncleanness is set into contrast with maddaf-uncleanness. In this instance the point is that the ^{c}am ha'ares) is unclean as a Zab. If a Zab shifts an object not used for sitting or lying, we know, the object suffers maddaf-uncleanness and renders food and drink unclean. M. Ed. 6:2 (Eliezer b. Hyrcanus. The Tradition and the Man [Leiden, 1973, I, p. 339-340]) further has a dispute of Joshua and Nehunya b. Elinathan with Eliezer, in which it is taken for granted, tangentially and within the structure of argument: "The uncleanness of living beings is greater than the uncleanness of corpses, for a living being imparts uncleanness, by lying and sitting, to what is underneath him, so that it conveys uncleanness to man and utensils, and also conveys maddaf-uncleanness to what is above him, so that it conveys uncleanness to food and liquid, a mode of transferring uncleanness which a corpse does not convey." The same authorities -- Joshua and Eliezer -- are at M. Par. 10:1-2, and, moreover, Yose continues the matter, at M. Toh. 8:2, taking the rule for granted, just as do Joshua and Eliezer. We need not review in detail Tosefta's usages of the same word, since all occur in the context of the correlative Mishnaic pericopae (T. Par. 10:2, 3, T. Toh. 9:4, T. Zab. 3:3, 5:1).

The two senses in which the word is used (now omitted: references to the occurrences in M. Kel.) of course are complementary. M. Par. and M. Toh. know maddaf as a status as to uncleanness contrasted to midras, and M. Zab. uses the word to refer to objects which can enter that very same status as to uncleanness. Our translation in the present tractate has been required by its context. But the meaning in point of fact is complementary to that necessitated by the context of M. Par. and M. Toh.: What can become unclean with maddaf-uncleanness -- an object not used for lying and sitting and hence not susceptible to midras-uncleanness (a point familiar throughout our order e.g., Kelim Chapter Twenty-Four) -- here is called maddaf. And M. Par. and M. Toh. know maddaf as that uncleanness imparted to something which can become unclean with maddaf-uncleanness, as distinct from something (used for lying and sitting) susceptible to midras. Our tractate, moreover, hastens to add: The status of maddaf-uncleanness is attained when an object not used for lying or sitting (also food or drink, explicitly included as well) is located above a Zab. Maddaf as the opposite of midras, of course, is contained in the pericopae of M. Toh. in particular, but also, with slight eisegesis, at M. Par.

The contrast between midras and maddaf, strikingly, is precisely the same the contrast as I have hypothetically imputed to the exegetes of Lev. 15:10 A at i, iii. Indeed, midras and maddaf express exactly the same idea as is spelled out above. Our invocation, at that point, of the rule of opposites therefore is justified by the result of the present analysis of the consistent contrast, drawn in M., between midras and maddaf. The concept of maddaf, in its two, complementary senses, most certainly is attested by Joshua and Eliezer at M. Ed. and M. Par. Because of the givenness of the idea of M. Par., at both pericopae assigned to Eliezer and Joshua, I am inclined to suppose that the concept of maddaf-uncleanness and of objects susceptible not to midras, because they are not used for lying and sitting, but, under the specified circumstance, to maddaf-uncleanness, hence maddaf-objects, originates before 70.

4. M. 5:6: He who touches the Zab, Zabah, menstruating woman, woman after childbirth, mesora[c], or a bed or chair on which any of these have lain or sat. Touching and shifting, carrying and being carried, are equivalent. + T. 5:3: utensils are in the first remove.	4. The pericope so far as it deals with modes of transfer makes two points. First, while one is touching these sources, he is able to impart uncleanness at two removes, unfitness at one. That is to say, just as at M. 5:1, he is like a Father of uncleanness, so far as food for heave-offering is concerned. Second, touching is deemed equivalent to shifting, carrying, and being carried.

That the uncleanness of the Zab is transferred to one who touches the Zab (etc.) is stated explicitly at Lev. 15:5. That one who carries such a thing is made unclean is stated at Lev. 15:10b.

The sole new point has to do with the inclusion of shifting as a mode of transfer of uncleanness. This is probably generated by the analogy to bearing the weight of the Zab, that is, carrying. The inclusion of shifting as a mode of transfer of uncleanness derives simply from the extension of Scripture's stated modes. One can hardly carry without shifting the object. The sole open question is whether we include even derivatives of the pressure of the Zab or of pressure upon the Zab, that is, vibration, movement which takes place indirectly and not directly. We do not, as the Ushans state.

5. M. 5:7: He who touches the flux of the Zab, his spit, his semen, his urine, and the blood of the menstruating woman (imparts uncleanness at two removes, etc.). All the same is touching and moving. Eliezer: Also carrying.

5.
1. The specified excretions are unclean just as the Zab is unclean.
2. They transfer uncleanness just as the Zab transfers uncleanness, that is, through contact.
3. Shifting is equivalent to contact.
4. Eliezer: Carrying is equivalent to contact.

Touching the spit of the Zab effects the transfer of the Zab's uncleanness, so Lev. 15:8. The secondary point is the inclusion of other substances. The issue of carrying as equivalent to contact of course is not of equivalent antiquity.

6. T. 5:2B: Phlegm, mucous, saliva, and snot of Zab are like his spit. Tear, blood of wound, milk of woman, blood of mouth and penis are unclean only in the first remove. Flux, spit, urine are unclean as Fathers. Semen of Zab: Eliezer -- does not impart uncleanness when carried; and sages -- imparts uncleanness when carried, because urine is contained therein.

Sifra Mesora^{c} Zabim 1:7-8: Zab imparts uncleanness through white flux, not through red flow blood from penis).

Sifra Mesora^{c} Zabim I:9-13: Flux itself is unclean. Blood which exudes from the penis is not unclean as flux. His urine is uncleanness. Sweat, rancid moisture, excrement are not unclean. Nine liquids apply to Zab: secretion, putrid sweat, excrement are clean in all respects; tear, blood, milk impart susceptibility to uncleanness as liquids; flux, spit, urine are unclean as flux.

Sifra Mesora^{c} Zabim 3:8: Phlegm, slaver, and snot are equivalent to spit.

Sifra Mesora^{c} Zabim 1:3: Flux derives solely from the genitals, not from the nose or mouth.

There are two issues in the present set, first of all, the notion that the transfer of the Zab's uncleanness takes place not solely through touching the Zab, but also through touching other substances which exude from him. Second, other modes of transfer besides direct contact are of the same effect as direct contact. The matter of touching the Zab's spit is explicit at Lev. 15:8. Accordingly, not only the flux, but also spit is unclean. Then spit supplies an analogy for other such substances which are like it. Flux is like semen; urine derives from the same location. Phlegm, mucus, saliva, snot, all are treated as analogous to spit. The second issue is the analogy between touching and moving, on which all parties agree. Eliezer wishes to treat carrying as equivalent mode of transfer of uncleanness. His basis, surely, will be the diverse rulings which treat touching, shifting, and carrying as equivalent. At T. 5:2B, an Eliezer wishes to exclude semen of the Zab. If this is the same Eliezer, then M. 5:7 should contain the equivalent qualification, that is, adding carrying as a mode of transfer of uncleanness, and detaching semen from the opening list. We do not know which Eliezer is before us, one of the Yavneans or one of the Ushans. That is why we cannot adduce the present set as evidence that discussion of the interrelationships of the diverse modes of transfer of uncleanness was carried forward at Yavneh, with the secondary notion that the issues were still live at that time. This is suggested by the pointed claim, intruded at M. 5:6, 7, etc., that the diverse modes do produce equivalent effects, or are the same as one another, which suggests that in the background are efforts seriously to distinguish among them. But the main point in Mishnah is that there are diverse modes, and that point derives from the obvious sense of Scripture, which specifies touching or contact, carrying, lying or sitting, generalized into exerting pressure.

7. M. 5:8: He who carries saddle, is carried on it, and moves it, etc.	7. Carrying, being carried on, and moving, the saddle imparts uncleanness as if one were made a Father of uncleanness.
Carrying carrion, purification water sufficient for sprinkling. + T. 5:5A.	Here, too, the man is as if he were a Father of uncleanness.

M. 5:9: He who eats carrion of clean bird, while it is in his gullet, etc.
+ T. 5:10-12.

This item is not relevant to Zabim.

Sifra Mesora^{c} Zabim 4:2-3: Bed and chair impart uncleanness when they are carried.

Sifra Mesora^{c} Zabim 4:1: Whoever touches saddle is unclean, but whoever touches what is under the saddle is not unclean on that account.

Carrying the saddle or being carried on it makes a person unclean, so Lev. 15:10 states explicitly. That the bed and chair which are carried impart uncleanness is also at Lev. 15:10b. Touching the saddle produces uncleanness, so Lev. 15:10a. Lev. 15:10b then specifies that whoever carries something which has been underneath a Zab is unclean, which then is exclusive of merely touching the saddle. Nothing in this set brings us significantly outside the boundaries of Scriptural meaning, so far as I can see. (We omit reference to the matter of carrion, which is not within the thematic limits of our tractate.)

8. M. 5:10: He who touches a dead creeping thing, semen, one made unclean by corpse-uncleanness, mesora^{c} during period of counting clean days, purification water insufficient for sprinkling, carrion, and saddle ...
This is the general rule: Whatever touches any of all the Fathers of uncleanness listed in the Torah imparts uncleanness at one remove and renders unfit at one. Man in contact with a Father of uncleanness imparts uncleanness at two removes, unfitness at one. Or: except for man, who, as a corpse, makes that which touches it into a Father of uncleanness and so that which is in contact with a corpse imparts uncleanness at two removes unfitness at one more.

8. In all these cases, the one who touches the source of uncleanness is unclean only in the first remove, not functioning as if he were a Father of uncleanness.

Any object, other than man, in contact with a Father of uncleanness, is in the first remove of uncleanness.

M. 5:11: He who has a seminal emission is like one who has touched a dead creeping thing. He who has sexual relations with a menstruating woman is like one who is unclean by reason of corpse-uncleanness, but he also imparts uncleanness to bed and chair so that they render food and drink unclean, which the former does not accomplish.

M. 5:12: Ten items which are in the second remove of uncleanness and therefore render heave-offering unfit. Sifra-Mesora[c] Zabim 2:8-13: Seminal emission does not cause uncleanness. Person unclean through nega[c], corpse, does not impart uncleanness to bed and chair.

The last units, M. 5:10-12, complete the construction of M. 5:6-9 by specifying sources of uncleanness, touching which leaves a person unclean only in the first remove, then in the second. The set contains no attestations, but in fact goes over the specifications of Scripture. What is pointed is the distinction between "whatever touches any of the Fathers of uncleanness" and "man who touches a Father of uncleanness," which is to say, the important point of M. 5:1, 6-9, upon which Joshua's further observation, about the difference between one's state while touching such a Father and after one has ceased to touch the Father, is based. The specification at Lev. 15:5, for the Zab, Lev. 15:21, for the menstruating woman, Lev. 15:27, for the Zab, and the comparison of the woman after childbirth to the menstruating woman, Lev. 12:2, 5, that the person who touches things on which the aforenamed have lain or sat washes his clothes, are what lead to the stated conclusion.

The Scriptural legacy upon which this tractate is based already has been described in detail. Part of the legacy to the authorities before 70, and, we have no reason to doubt, to the authorities who come even before the Houses after the turn of the first century A.D., certainly has been specified in my account of the clear implication of Scripture; another part is likely to be contained within what we have deemed the secondary meaning of Scripture. The origin of the terminology, e.g., midras and maddaf, is not equivalently clear, nor can we be certain that the homogenization of diverse forms of pressure under the term, midras, and its differentiation, as at M. 2:4, into diverse acts, all of which produce midras-uncleanness, are equally early. In any event so far as we claim to account for the history of the legal ideas of Zabim, we simply allege that whatever Scripture states explicitly, and much that is derived from Scripture merely by generalizing on details given in Scripture, form the fundamental antecedents to the work of the Houses and others in the period before 70. Of greater weight, as at Niddah, Zabim commences its development not in Scripture but among that group which determined to take seriously, therefore to study with great care, Scripture on the subject of the Zab. That group or circle self-evidently takes shape before the turn of the first century A.D., but we have no way of estimating the time at which it did its work on this tractate or on any other.

The upshot for the inquiry at hand is now self-evident. Since we can account for the generative facts of the tractate by replicating the processes of exegetical reasoning at hand, we uncover no evidence of a source of facts ("truth") other than the written Scripture. No independent tradition underlies ideas or facts contained within unassigned sayings, no "oral Torah" distinct from, and autonomous of, the "written Torah." Unassigned sayings do bear the generative notions of the tractate at hand, but they get their ideas from Scripture, as I have demonstrated. So far as the "oral Torah" is supposed to stand independent of the written one, no "oral Torah" stands behind this tractate. But so far as the "oral Torah" is alleged to rest upon the written one and states its secondary exegetical message, the tractate at hand sustains such a theory.

If other tractates produced similar types of unattributed traditions, and if these unattributed traditions formed a distinct group and also bore the burden of the presuppositions of the tractate at hand, and if the presuppositions then could be linked to the principal secondary and tertiary factual allegations of the tractate, then the theory of the unattributed saying in relationship to the "oral Torah" of which the Mishnah is alleged to form a principal expression would find substantiation. As it is, the tractate before us is interesting because it, in context, is unique in its division (and, in point of fact, among all five dozen tractates of the Mishnah).

CHAPTER ELEVEN
TEBUL YOM

i. Unattributed Pericopae

The present catalogue lists pericopae which cannot be clearly assigned to a particular circle or stratum upon the basis of internal attribution or external attestation. I discern no unattributed pericope which cannot be linked through common conception to another pericope, the latter bearing clear evidence of attribution or attestation.

[1. M. 2:1-2: The principle that the Tebul Yom does not make liquids unclean is taken for granted by Eliezer, Joshua, at M. Toh. 8:7/T. T.Y. 1:8-10. The view that liquids which exude from him are in the same status is secondary. + T. 1:3, 4-10.]

[2. M. 2:4, T. 2:1: The principle is exactly the same as at M. 2:3, which is Ushan.]

[3. M. 2:8: Attested to Usha by T. 2:5.]

[4. T. 2:11: Goes over Aqiba's conception at M. 3:4-5.]

[5. M. 4:1-3: The principle that the Tebul Yom is unclean in the second remove is certainly prior to the earliest attributed rulings. Joshua attests at T. 2:14.]

[6. M. 4:4: Illustrates M. 4:1-3's principle and especially the cleanness which is completed at sunset.]

ii. Tebul Yom before 70

There is no usable evidence on this issue.

iii. From Mishnah to Scripture

Scripture is unambiguous about the status of that which has been put in water. It is unclean until the evening. It is the principle, surely deriving from the period before the turn of the first century, that the immersion-pool for forty seahs of still water effects purification, which much later raises the ambiguity. The history of the law is in two stages of unequal size. The Yavneans know, Joshua's gloss suggests, that the Tebul Yom is in the second remove of uncleanness, imparting unfitness to heave-offering. The Ushans then ask whether that means what has been immersed is really unclean until evening, therefore falling into the same status as all other sources of uncleanness in regard to connection. Or is what has been immersed really clean, therefore imparting unfitness to heave-offering in accord with the distinction important to Ushans between what is primary and what is secondary? The sequence of ideas on the Tebul Yom is encompassed by these correlative matters, essential cleanness and distinction in regard to connection, or essential uncleanness and no such distinction. The tractate on the Tebul Yom is self-contained, imposing upon itself a remarkably limited intellectual agendum. None of this derives from Scripture.

CHAPTER TWELVE
YADAYIM

i. Unattributed Sayings

The only item clearly lacking an attested or attributed parallel is No. 6, which is, however, a notion hardly surprising in the light of M. Miq. Chapters Nine and Ten. The principle, No. 8, that holy writings impart uncleanness to hands is taken for granted in pericopae attributed to Joshua and other Yavneans. I am inclined to see it as deriving from the period before 70. The other entries indicate the grounds for assigning to a particular stratum items lacking clearcut attributions or attestations internal to the law as presently formulated.

[1. T. 1:5: Cleaning hands for sanctuary requires a quarter-log. Conforms to Yose's view, M. 1:1, but Meir may concur.]

[2. M. 1:2/T. 1:6-9: Utensils must be used for water for washing hands. This is wholly unassigned. M. Par. 5:5-9 is Ushan, however, and this set is also apt to belong to that stratum. See Part IX, pp. 144-145. The matter has no Yavnean antecedents.]

[3. T. 1:10B-11/M. 1:5A: Attested in principle to Usha by M. 1:4.]

[4. T. 1:12/M. 1:5C: T. goes over the ground of M., which is Ushan.]

[5. M. 2:2A-F/T. 2:5, 6; + M. 2:3/T. 1:3A, 2:1, 2, 3A, 4, 7, 8: T. illustrates the notion that the second water purifies the first water on the hands -- but only on the hands. Develops the issue of Meir vs. Yose.]

*6. T. 1:4: Whatever interposes on the body interposes on the hands.

[7. M. 2:4/T. 1:15-18: Matters of doubt deemed clean. Attested to Usha by Yose.]

[8. M. 4:5 + T. 2:10, 12, 13: Scroll which wore out but contains eighty-five letters. Attested by M. 3:4-5. The conception that holy writings impart uncleanness to hands is taken for granted at Yavneh, M. 3:2 + 4:6; the definitions are Yavneh and Ushan.]

ii. Yadayim before 70

There is no evidence pertinent to this matter.

iii. From Mishnah to Scripture

There is no scriptural foundation for this tractate.

CHAPTER THIRTEEN
UQSIN

i. Unattributed Sayings

The present catalogue lists items not clearly attributed to particular authorities yet well attested by them, as well as materials lacking evidence of a particular point of congruence or even relevance.

[1. M. 1:1: The principles of M. are attested at Usha by M. 2:2-4. Eleazar b. ^{C}Azariah, M. 1:5, knows that what serves the produce is deemed connected, thus the principle of M. 1:1B. There is, along these same lines, no reason to assign the matter of the handle as connected to the time after Yavneh. + T. 1:1-4: Ushan attributions also attest the principles of unattributed entries.]

[2. M. 1:5C-K: The principles is attested to Yavneh by Eleazar b. ^{C}Azariah. (Compare M. Toh. 3:1, 10:5.)]

[3. M. 2:2: All pits contract, transmit uncleanness, join together -- contradicted by M. 2:2B-F, which is attested to Usha by T. 2:1.]

[4. T. 2:4: Continues T. 2:2-3, which are attested by Rabbi.]

[5. T. 2:9 Shells of beans, if they contain food-matter, receive uncleanness as foods. Likely to be Ushan, along the lines of M. 2:4.]

[6. M. 2:5A-C: Attested by Rabbi, T. 2:7 + T. 2:8B.]

[7. M. 2:5D-F: Attested by Ben ^{C}Azzai, T. 2:13 + T. 2:15A.]

[8. T. 1:7: Connection effected by man is null. Attested to Usha at T. Oh. 4:8.]

*9. T. 1:8A: Dough kneaded with fruit-juice is insusceptible.

*10. M. 2:6, T. 2:15B, 2:16A. Shell of roasted egg is connected until chipped, and further definitions.

*11. M. 2:8, T. 2:8A: Re measuring bulk of leaves with sap; leaves with empty space.

[12. M. 3:1-3, 9, T. 3:1-3, 4-5: This unit is admirably attested to Usha by M. 3:2F-H, 3:3H, etc.]

[13. M. 3:4A-B, T. 3:9: Attested to Usha by Simeon.]

[14. M. 3:8H, T. 2:11, 12B: The issue is Ushan.]

The problem of No. 10 is familiar in numerous attested pericopae. No. 11 is certainly secondary to the matter of the requisite bulk of vegetables for imparting uncleanness. There are no considerable conceptions which do not relate to legal principles adequately attested, in the main, to Usha. The problem of unattributed sayings is trivial and peripheral to this tractate. The unattributed sayings do not form a distinct group, separate from the attributed ones. They also do not contain basic ideas that generate secondary disputes in attributed sayings, as Yose's allegation at T. San. would lead us to anticipate.

ii. Uqsin before 70

There is no relevant material.

iii. From Mishnah to Scripture

The issue of this tractate is philosophical. The theme of Uqsin is uncleanness of food. Its problematic is the interrelationships of various parts of a given piece of fruit or vegetable. And the recurrent and interesting side of that problematic is Judah's (the Houses', Aqiba's) interest in whether, if we begin to pull a piece of fruit or vegetable apart, the as-yet-undetached parts of said piece of fruit or vegetable are deemed integral and thus "attached," or, because it is inevitable that they be detached, are they deemed already detached. That issue pertains to many other legal themes, it goes without saying, and is not religio-legal but philosophical in character, as a moment of thought on the relationship between the acorn and the oak, or between what is potential and what is actual, will suggest. Accordingly, the legal raw materials of the tractate once more are shown to be reworked into the framework of perennial philosophical concerns, and, as at M. Tohorot, the uncleanness of food is made to address matters of metaphysics. This is the trait of the Ushan thinkers in particular. It is they who transformed religious taboos into philosophical ideas, transcending their inheritance of trivial rules and petty obsessions by both preserving the substantive nature of, and imparting a wholly intellectual new character to, those rules and obsessions. The history of the Mishnaic law of purities is the story of the movement not from Scripture to Mishnah but of mind and thought from religion to philosophy.

CHAPTER FOURTEEN
CONCLUSION

i. The Problem of the Unattributed Sayings Reconsidered

At this advanced stage in the work, it is difficult to recall that, at the outset, the issue of unattributed sayings and how these are to be "dated," or assigned to specific strata, seemed urgent. Indeed, the present labor began with the intention of reckoning with the compelling problem of unattributed sayings. As in many tractates, there is simply no problem. There are conceptions everywhere taken for granted and assigned to no authority; these go back before 70 and constitute the intellectual foundation -- such as it is -- of some tractates. But for the materials we do have -- the actual sayings constructed into pericopae -- we have almost nothing lacking evidence, of substantial and weighty value, on the appropriate stratum for assignment.

I am inclined to think that, in any event, the problem is falsely phrased. The really interesting and unanswerable question is how to locate the intellectual father[s] of a tractate, the people who determined its largest and encompassing traits, the issues to be worked out, the logical and generative principles behind specific pericopae and mooted opinions. For these traits derive from people not mentioned in the assigned materials. What we do have in the names of specific authorities is generally discussion of secondary and tertiary matters of detail, gray areas of law left open for discussion after all the really decisive issues had been settled. These decisions give a tractate its generative principle, its shape and intellectual form. We do not know who made the fundamental distinctions, on the one side, or who determined how these generative conceptions would be developed (or, in point of fact, left nearly wholly undeveloped) on the other. Just as tractates exhibit preferences, chapter by chapter, for disciplined forms, so do they leave no doubt whatsoever about their foci of interest, predominant concerns, and methods of articulation of the law. Who laid down the agendum for a tractate? Answers to such a question cannot derive from a tractate's universal tendency to attribute specific teachings to named authorities, simply because what is given in the names of said authorities is trivial and, from the viewpoint of the underlying modes of thought, highly contingent.

Why then the urgency of the question, How do we know that the authority to whom a saying is attributed really said it? In the analysis of the intellectual history of the law, the logical development of its principles and unfolding of its themes, it is important to know what came first, what followed later on. It is not equally important to know whether specific authorities said what they are supposed to have said, which is a separate question. The reason is that in relationship to the intellectual history of the law, that information will tell us nothing we do not already know, nothing we must know for the central task. If a saying is given to an authority before 70 and is taken for granted and even revised and developed by a saying attributed to an authority later on, then we have reason to claim to know how the law unfolded. What additional and necessary information do we have when we know who stands behind its unfolding? We know something more about said authority, but nothing more about the law itself, so far as I can discern.

To be sure, the Amoraic exegetes of the law raise the issue of which second-century master stands behind a given, anonymous rule. The purpose of their inquiry, however, is not biographical but logical and legal. They wish to discern whether consistency can be uncovered between a principle known to be held by an authority and one which seems also to have been maintained by him. Their interest is in the interrelationship of autonomous and discrete rules, the underlying connections between them. This interest is well served by definition of the inquiry in terms of individuals. But it is simply not a biographical matter, even though it is phrased in biographical categories.

Accordingly, what we do not know and never can find out, namely, whether a given authority really said what is assigned to him, hardly impedes the inquiry into what we do want to know. This goal is the history of the religious ideas of Rabbinic Judaism in its earliest stages, therefore the history of the specific and concrete laws, organized by tractates, in which these ideas are encapsulated. To the extent that full and nuanced history includes attention to which notions derive from what authorities or circles, the best we are able to do is admit the limitations of our information. That is to say, we claim only that, in the time the law was taking shape, a given saying was believed to have been laid down -- in principle or in substance, if not in the exact wording -- by the specific authority who is named. As I said, we cannot evaluate the accuracy of that belief or allegation.

It is from New Testament scholars that we learn urgently to ask whether what is supposed to have been done really happened, whether what is alleged to have been said by a given master really was said by him. But we have moved far beyond these questions, with which, admittedly, the critical work begins. Indeed, in retrospect we see that the primary value of these particular questions was in properly evaluating the work of earlier historians of the Jews and Judaism in late antiquity, and, in particular, that of those many historians who take for granted the literal veracity of texts. These commit the act of fundamentalism, in its intellectually most vulgar form, upon texts of exquisite subtlety and intellectual delicacy, even of poetry and surpassing conceptual beauty. It is in moving beyond the limits of established, and wrong, suppositions that the New Testament lessons proved valuable, as I said. Yet, it now is clear, we do not need to learn from those particular scholars the vital and liberating lessons of a critical stance toward the sources. Scholars of Tanakh teach the same lessons, and in a much less tendentious spirit.

For New Testament scholars pursue questions weighty with salvific implication. The information is meant to answer theological questions. If it could be shown that the chief authority of their documents did or did not say what is assigned to him, important implications for the shape of faith and its contemporary form and message emerge. History is meant as a vehicle of reform. The historical arena is to be filled with theological contestants. The gnostic character of the inquiry -- the pursuit not of mere knowledge but of salvific knowledge -- invests scholarly arguments with unfortunate and inappropriate considerations. I do not need to elaborate the point that, whether or not Aqiba or Meir really said what is attributed to him bears no consequences whatever for contemporary Judaism or even for the shape of the practical, practiced law. It has no bearing on the life of Torah. I shall not eat pork no matter what Meir "really" said or did not say. This work, which began in response to the correct and vivifying questions of New Testament scholars, has now therefore to proceed beyond the limits of its original agendum, to specify its own purposes and directions.

Let me now answer the questions with which this survey got under way (above):

1. In the average, something like 10% of the whole of the Mishnah's and Tosefta's tractates in the division of Purities may be constituted by unattributed sayings. But in some tractates the percentage is 1% or 2%. For the Mishnah alone, separate from the Tosefta, the proportion is still smaller. Accordingly, we must conclude, the problem of the unattributed saying in quantity is negligible.

2. In character and quality, excluding tractate Zabim, ideas presented in unattributed sayings cannot be differentiated from those in named ones. Unattributed sayings, for instance, do not consistently treat problems of a single character, e.g., importance, nor are they ordinarily focused upon matters of tertiary detail. The character and quality of the contents of unattributed sayings do not permit description and analysis through a set of criteria differentiated from those serviceable for the contents of attributed ones.

3. Only rarely do we find ideas or facts taken for granted in unattributed sayings that stand at the logical beginning of the unfolding of the principles and propositions of a given tractate. Where we do find <u>only</u> in unattributed sayings facts that are critical to the ideational structure of a exegesis by stages of analogical and contrastive reasoning to reconstruct the thought-patterns by which, out of facts of Scripture, facts at the foundation of the Mishnah were elicited. (This is particularly critical to the history of the ideational structure of Niddah and Zabim.) By definition those two facts form a secondary expansion of the written Torah, not a sherd of the "oral" one, if the latter is supposed to be autonomous of the former.

4. It follows that as a group unattributed ideas do not form a bridge from the Mishnah back to Scripture (let alone from the Tosefta anywhere). When we contemplate the unattributed sayings, in no way need we call to mind the myth of the dual Torah and explain that at hand is that missing link between the written and the Oral Torah.

ii. <u>From Mishnah to Scripture</u>

Yet, the fact remains that the Mishnah is identified by its heirs and continuators in Judaism as the corner-stone of the Oral Torah. While the myth turns out not to rest upon facts of literature or history, it constitutes a profound judgment upon the phenomenology of the Mishnah in relationship to Scripture. It is so profound and accurate, indeed, that, in the context of the history of religion, we may indeed affirm the myth as a deep statement of truth. That is to say, the Mishnah indeed constitutes the written-down version of the Oral Torah. In what way? The Mishnah complements and completes the written Torah, yet stands aloof and alone from the written Torah. Let me now explain.

We must first distinguish the three tractates which deal with sources of uncleanness, Negaim, Niddah, and Zabim, from those which deal with the locus of uncleanness and with the removal of uncleanness, Kelim, the shank of Ohalot, Parah, Miqvaot, and the rabbinical tractates, Tohorot and Makhshirin. When we review the first four, we see that their fundamental and generative conceptions bear no resemblance to anything laid down in the Priestly Code, although the articulation of details of the law responds to specific verses of Scripture. The last two, Tohorot and Makhshirin, in any event begin after 70 and either ignore Scripture or utterly reverse its implications by introducing considerations undreamt of in the Priestly Code. Zabim, Niddah, and Negaim, by contrast, all spin out Scriptural conceptions, with scarcely a single generative idea, let alone fundamental presupposition, not explicitly stated within the Priestly Code.

Kelim begins in the original conception that utensils not in the Temple and not for use in the cult are subject to uncleanness. Neither Scripture nor the exegesis of Scripture generated that revolutionary conception (Purities Part III, pp. 383-4). The prologue of Ohalot (M. Oh. 1:1-3:5) deals with things which contaminate in the tent, or through overshadowing, and the epilogue (M. Oh. 16:3-18:10) with graveyards, thus grounds or substances which contaminate as does the corpse. Nothing in these sections on sources of uncleanness equivalent to the corpse does more than extend and fill out the Scriptural rule of corpse-uncleanness itself. Accordingly, laws on sources of corpse-uncleanness in the opening and closing parts of Ohalot stand upon the foundation of Scripture, with remarkably little exegesis. When, however, we deal with the shank of the tractate, M. 3:6-16:2, and turn to the subtle interplay between the Tent and the utensil, we leave the Scriptural domain entirely. Not a single concept or presupposition derives directly or indirectly from the exegesis of Scripture. The proposition that corpse-uncleanness passes through a handbreadth of open space and its passage may be prevented by a handbreadth of closed space, which stands behind every major and formative conception of the shank of Ohalot, is autonomous. The obvious difference is that the prologue and epilogue deal with sources of uncleanness, and the body of the tractate, with the locus, the definition of the Tent affected by the corpse (Part V, pp. 225-234).

Parah presents a noteworth contrast to Scripture. Num. 19:1-20 take for granted that the rite of burning the red cow is conducted in a state of uncleanness, since it is not performed in the tent of meeting. Participating in the rite makes a person unclean. Parah by contrast assumes that a high degree of cleanness characterizes all those who participate in the rite as well as utensils used therein. The tractate spells out the requirements of cleanness in preparing the ash, drawing the water, and participating in the cult (Part I, pp. xi-xii). Parah deals not with sources of uncleanness, but with the locus of cleanness (Part I, pp. 220-222). The cleanness-rules of Parah create in the world outside the cult a place of cleanness analogous to the cult. The main point of the Priestly Code is that for cultic purposes purification is attained through the application of blood, or through immersion in living water, or through sunset. But for purification Miqvaot speaks only of immersion in the appropriate pool, or, self-evidently, a flowing stream. Miqvaot accepts immersion in a pool of water, the natural properties of which have not been affected by human agency. Since the purpose of immersion is the attainment of cultic purity, they take a position quite outside that imagined in Scripture. In Parah we create a place for a sacrifice outside of the Temple, a place of cleanness and holiness. In Miqvaot we call into being a means of attaining cleanness outside of the Temple, a kind of water not used for the Temple described in the Priestly Code. Spring water (which serves as well) is different from rain water. The one is exceptional, the other ordinary, the one flows with force, the other stands still, the one (Miqvaot says) cleans in any amount, the other serves the body or the utensil only in the volume of forty seahs. The spring water, which can purify for the cult and for the table alike, therefore has traits quite distinct from the sort of water which serves for the table. That is as it should be, for the difference between the altar of the Temple and the table of the home, both to be clean, to be sure, is not to be obscured (Part XIV, pp. 193-205).

Two tractates deal not with the sources of uncleanness but with the processes, the affects upon food and drink, of the several sources of uncleanness. Both begin their history after 70 and both express deeply rabbinical concerns. Tractate Tohorot bears no close tie to Scripture at all (Part XII, p. 2). True, an effort is made to ground rules on removes of uncleanness, in particular of unconsecrated food, in Scriptural exegesis. But the exegesis is blatantly post facto; no claim is made that the exegesis goes back to hoary antiquity. It is difficult to see that the legal achievements of Yavneh and Usha rest upon a considerable antecedent corpus of laws or even of principles. It looks to me as though the primary contribution of the authorities before 70 to Tohorot is the general notion that cleanness applies to foods and liquids consumed outside of the Temple. In the matter of removes of uncleanness as related to degrees of sanctification of such food, the clear evidence is that the issue is first investigated after 70. Opinions attributed to Yavneans contain the basic suppositions, and these are under dispute. Most of the pericopae of Tohorot on doubts in connection with uncleanness are assigned to Ushans. Similarly, with respect to how people who keep cleanness-rules deal with those who do not, we may suppose that before 70 some sort of corpus of principles may have existed, for the problem begins when a few people undertake to keep the laws among many who do not. But the systematization of principles is not all that the Ushans have accomplished. They also appear to set down principles, because they debate the most fundamental questions on the relationship between the ᶜam ha'ares and the haver.

While Makhshirin depends upon the datum of Scripture (Lev. 11:24, 38) that produce is susceptible to uncleanness only when it is wet, that tractate begins in an interest absent in Scripture, which is in the character of the liquid which imparts wetness, therefore susceptibility to uncleanness, and in the way in which the liquid happens to come upon produce. In fact, the tractate's first principle, its distinction between liquids which do and do not impart susceptibility to uncleanness, derives from circles including Aqiba, and its second principle, the distinction between intentional and unintentional wetting down, assuredly comes to us from Aqiba, in a direct line from Abba Yose-Joshua. The tractate as a whole begins its major conceptual development with Aqiba. What forms its center and unifies its diverse pericopae into a single, remarkably coherent document is the thought of Aqiba on the principal role of human intention in activating the supernatural forces of uncleanness, a view which does not begin in, and is not produced by exegesis of, Scripture (Part XVII, pp. 1-6, 178-222). We therefore notice once more that what the foregoing tractates have in common is an interest in the locus of uncleanness and the processes by which uncleanness affects and is removed from that locus.

We now come to the three tractates which give laws of *sources* of uncleanness. Negaim contains not a single generative idea except for the distinction between *nega*^{c} and *sara*^{c}*at*, which, once drawn, makes no difference whatsoever in the articulation of the law (Part VIII, p. xii). Negaim, which provides an account of one source of unclean- ness, follows, except where it improves upon, the thematic agendum of Leviticus Chapters Thirteen and Fourteen (Part VI, pp. 2-18, Part VIII, p. 221). No primary theme or supposition of Mishnah diverges from what is explicit in Scripture. True, *nega*^{c} and *sara*^{c}*at* are separate diseases, with the former laid under the examination of the rabbi. But in no way does *nega*^{c} as a source of uncleanness differ from *sara*^{c}*at* as a source of uncleanness (Part VIII, pp. 244-250). When we first encountered the fact that Scripture and Mishnah simply go over the same ground, we found it difficult to account for because of contrary results for Kelim and Ohalot (Part VIII, pp. 257-8). Negaim then seemed to present an exception to a well-established rule of the autonomy of Mishnah, Oral Torah, from the Priestly Code, Written Torah. The law of Niddah begins in Scripture and rises in necessarily sequential and logical stages therefrom. Accordingly, the laws of that tractate clearly begin at the point at which someone determined to undertake a careful reading of Scripture on the matter of Niddah and draw practical consequences from the results of that reading. There is not a single principle which Scripture does not supply. In Niddah we do not discover a single central conception of Mishnah which stands apart from, let alone at variance with, the Written Torah. Mishnah serves essentially to fill out areas opened, but left undefined, by Scripture (Part XVI, pp. 1-6, 194-211).

Accordingly, the three tractates, Negaim, Niddah, and Zabim, devoted to the materials of Leviticus Chapters Twelve, Thirteen, Fourteen, and Fifteen, those chapters of the Priestly Code which specify sources of uncleanness apart from unclean creates, and M. Ohalot Chapters One-Three and Sixteen-Eighteen, bear a single relationship to Scripture. All begin in the Scriptural conceptions as to the uncleanness of the *mesora*^{c}, the menstruating women, the Zabah, the Zab, the woman after childbirth, and the corpse. Among the sources of major uncleanness mentioned in the Priestly Code, Mishnah treats these at great length and in much detail. What the tractates have in common is that none of them innovates in any regard. All of them draw out tendencies and implications of Scripture. In their fundamental and generative conceptions, they constitute little more than secondary and derivative developments of the conceptions of the Priestly Code. By contrast, the tractates which define objects susceptible to uncleanness, areas in which, and processes by which, uncleanness takes place, and modes of purification from uncleanness contracted by such objetsqq and in such areas, all have in common the simple fact that Scripture contributes little of generative consequence.

The Mishnah therefore is autonomous and distinct from Scripture in respect to two dimensions of the tripartite realm of purity: (1) sources of uncleanness (including modes of transfer of uncleanness), (2) objects of uncleanness (including food and drink), and (3) means for the removal of uncleanness. The Mishnah is entirely dependent for its principles upon the Scripture in regard to sources of uncleanness. The Oral Torah -- the Mishnah's Division of Purities -- does not contain a single new source of major uncleanness. Apart from adding analogous substances and the idol, it scarcely specifies any object or substance or person or status which generates major uncleanness. Nothing causes major uncleanness which Scripture itself does not declare to be a major source of uncleanness. (M. Zab. 5:10-12 are clear on this point.)

What the Oral Torah wishes to say in completion of "the whole Torah of Moses, our Rabbi," is that the locus of cleanness, therefore also of uncleanness, is in the world beyond the cult. World completes cult. The lines of structure emanating from the Temple encompass all reality. The table at home must be as clean as the altar in the Temple must be clean. Domestic utensils have therefore in principle to be divided between those susceptible, and those insusceptible to uncleanness. The utensils subject to corpse-uncleanness (Num. 19:15) are distinguished from the Tent of the corpse. Means of attaining cleanness outside the cult, water, and a locus of cleanness even for sacrifice outside the cult, the place in which the rite of the red cow is conducted, are beautifully constructed. The complex rules governing food and drink are worked out a Tohorot and Makhshirin.

The Written Torah's system of uncleanness and cleanness is augmented and enriched by the Oral Torah, not revised or overturned. Nothing declared by the Written Torah to be a source of uncleanness is held to be clean in the Oral Torah. The Oral Torah adds to the sources of uncleanness specified in the Written one only analogous substances (excluding the idol, about which P knows nothing). The difference in the relationship to Scripture of the two groups of tractates, Negaim-Niddah-Zabim, on the one side, Kelim, the shank of Ohalot, Parah, Tohorot, Miqvaot, Makhshirin, on the other, accordingly begins in the distinctive and fresh perspectives of the authorities who, some time before the turn of the first century A.D., brought to the Priestly code a peculiarly priestly interest in the analogy between sacred and secular, Temple and world, cultic altar and domestic table. Aptly might a Pharisee have said, "Think not that I have come to abolish the (priestly) Law. I have come not to abolish but to fulfil it." And appropriate to the Division of Purities is the later rabbinical view of Mishnah as a whole: the Oral Torah indeed forms the complement and completion of the Written Torah, the dual Torah which is "the <u>one</u> whole Torah of Moses, our Rabbi."

INDEX